D0231574

The Great War
on the
Western Front

The Great War on the Western Front

A Short History

Paddy Griffith

Pen & Sword

MILITARY

First published in Great Britain in 2008 by
PEN & SWORD MILITARY
an imprint of
Pen & Sword Books Ltd
47 Church Street
Barnsley
South Yorkshire
S70 2AS

Copyright © Paddy Griffith, 2008

ISBN 978-1-84415-764-8

Typeset by Concept, Huddersfield, West Yorkshire
Printed and bound in Great Britain by Biddles Ltd

Pen & Sword Books Ltd incorporates the imprints of
Pen & Sword Aviation, Pen & Sword Maritime, Pen & Sword Military,
Wharncliffe Local History, Pen & Sword Select,
Pen & Sword Military Classics and Leo Cooper.

For a complete list of Pen & Sword titles please contact
PEN & SWORD BOOKS LIMITED
47 Church Street, Barnsley, South Yorkshire, S70 2AS, England.
E-mail: enquiries@pen-and-sword.co.uk
Website: www.pen-and-sword.co.uk

Contents

The Great War on the Western Front

List of Maps and Illustrations

List of Plates

Lord Kitchener of Khartoum recruiting his New Armies in 1914.

British troops conducting naively amateurish training in Scotland, 1914.

Too many French attacks in 1914 were defeated with heavy casualties when they failed to co-ordinate artillery support for their massed infantry.

A light German field gun being manhandled into action, 1914.

The famous French 'soixante quinze' 75mm quick-firing field gun, which had revolutionized artillery in 1900 but was already too light for the needs of 1914.

Three British officers dining in their snug dugout.

Indian troops at Fauquissart Post, Ypres area. Two Indian divisions were consumed on the Western Front in the winter of 1914–15, and not replaced.

Gurkhas with their fearsome kukris (fighting knives) near Neuve Chapelle in March 1915.

Soldiers with some of the new technology of trench warfare in the muzzles of their rifles, in the form of rifle grenades and wire cutters.

Chinese labourers at work on the British lines of communication: a vital but unsung resource.

French troops in the steep, stony and snowy terrain of the high Vosges.

The Great War on the Western Front

Dragging up a big gun by hand, illustrating the poor mobility of artillery on the muddy battlefields of 1916.

Walking wounded British and German soldiers on the Somme, 1916.

'La Voie Sacrée' at Verdun in 1916: the vital road along which an endless column of motor lorries kept the garrison supplied.

The heroism of the trenches, 1916: this man was credited with rescuing twenty of his wounded comrades.

The small comforts of trench life, 1916: the 'Café Royal' canteen.

An infantry patrol crawling through wire and *chevaux de frise* around Beaumont Hamel, 1916.

President Poincaré and Marshal Joffre visit officers' quarters on the Somme, 1916.

Mining at Messines in 1916, in preparation for the battle in 1917. By this time the mine had been perfected as a technology for static warfare.

Training model of terrain at Messines, before the battle of June 1917. Careful briefing was a vital part of the 'rehearsal' phase in any battle.

A British advance in 1917, leaving typically shallow trenches.

A typical trench scene in 1917: British troops sleeping in mud holes.

A classic view of the tortured moonscape of the Western Front, showing how clearly the trenches could be mapped from the air.

A forlorn plea to conserve ammunition, at a time when the British alone were firing off around a million shells per week.

Vickers machine gun engaged in long-range 'barrage' fire at Arras, 1917. This was an innovative technique for supplementing an artillery barrage.

Ancient meets modern: airpower shares the battlefield with French cavalry whose sabres are drawn but whose carbines are slung.

List of Plates

Canadians with a captured pillbox at Ypres, 1917. The Germans were at least a year ahead of the allies in the use of concrete for fortification.

German troops in tactical pose at La Vacquerie, 1917.

US cemetery at Belleau Wood, where American troops halted the German Aisne offensive in June 1918.

US infantry at bayonet drill: an atavistic practice that was often mocked in this war of high explosives and advanced machinery.

General 'Black Jack' Pershing awarding congressional medals of honor at Chaumont, 1918.

3,000 of America's three million troops in France, 1918. This major new infusion of manpower would have been decisive if the war had continued into 1919.

A German machine gun team in the front line, 1918.

One of the very few German-built tanks, in September 1918. It was a mechanically execrable design.

A British Whippet (light and relatively fast) tank, during a muddy phase of the 'Hundred Days' in late 1918.

French 320mm railway guns in action, 1918. France was two years behind the central powers in the production of super-heavy artillery, but she caught up in the end.

The 'Strassenkampf', or civil war on the streets, in Berlin, late 1918.

Field Marshal Haig leading the British Empire troops in the Paris Victory March, 14 July 1919.

Acknowledgements

Illustrations have been supplied by the Taylor Library, Barnsley, unless otherwise acknowledged. I am grateful to Ed Dovey for drawing the maps on pp. 14 and 89.

Preface

Very many large, laudable and learned books have been written about the Western Front, but there are not nearly as many of them as there are sensationalist and subjective ones. The present volume hopes to fall into neither of those two categories, but to present a short and compact overview that is accessible to the general reader, and which may serve as a springboard for further reading. It is also intended to offer a mainly 'military' explanation of what happened, including the place of the Western Front in the general history of 'the art of war'. This means that on one hand we will not look closely at the higher diplomacy, politics and strategy of the war as a whole, nor at the evolution of other fronts. On the other hand we will leave to others the task of interpreting the horrors, the traumas and the poetry of trench life.

My narrative deals mainly with the English-speaking armies on the Western Front – the British, Australians, Canadians, New Zealanders, South Africans and Americans – although I hope that the Germans and French will not be relegated to the status merely of 'walk-on parts'. Obviously during the period before 1 July 1916 it was those two nations which fought by far the major part of the war in the West, and they continued to fight many major battles with each other, without large-scale Anglo-Saxon intervention, right up to the very end. Nevertheless it remains true that the war entered a very different phase when the British 'New Armies' entered the fray in force on the Somme in the summer of 1916. Both the modernity and the intensity of the fighting would grow inexorably during the next two years, as the allies became stronger and the Germans gradually wilted. There would be setbacks along the way, notably the German spring offensives of 1918, but it was clear that France no longer stood alone, and would eventually clear the invader out of her lands.

Paddy Griffith
Withington, May 2007

CHAPTER ONE

The Start of the War and of the Western Front

The Start of the War and of the Western Front

THE START OF THE WAR

It would be a grotesque understatement to say that the First World War represented a major turning point in history. Four great empires were brought down by it – the German, Russian, Austro-Hungarian and Ottoman empires – while those that remained were battered beyond recognition. An array of awesome new weaponry, mass-produced on an industrial scale, killed over 10 million people within the space of four years, quite apart from what must have amounted to some 20 million maimed and injured, and doubtless even more. Nor could the damage be limited 'merely' to that, because the botched peace treaties of 1919 would lead on to a second and still worse world war just twenty years later, which would kill over 60 million.

At least the rights and wrongs of the Second World War would be relatively straightforward and easy to understand. With the First (or 'Great') War this is considerably less easy to say. It has a reputation as a 'futile' war which began for no particularly good reason, and continued with shifting and ambiguous objectives for each combatant nation. There were no great ideologies in conflict, such as Fascism versus Communism or Democracy versus Dictatorship, but only a set of squabbling old-fashioned imperialisms and nationalisms which to the modern outsider do not seem to have been worth the gigantic price that was paid to sustain them. To the modern eye it seems that the inefficient monarchies and incomplete democracies of 1914 marched off to war far too readily, blindly following long-ingrained habits whereby the impoverished and deferential masses would spring to arms enthusiastically, whenever the emperors and their general staffs chose to click their fingers.

However, if viewed in a different light we can see that the real issue at stake was whether or not Germany should be allowed to impose hegemony over the whole of continental Europe, and thereby emerge as the first true 'superpower' in the global arena. In 1914 Germany was already the strongest military power in the world, and stopping her would inevitably be a titanic undertaking. Not even the whole 'Entente Cordiale' of France, Russia, Britain and eventually Italy possessed adequate military power to have any realistic hope of a

The Great War on the Western Front

quick and easy victory, although unrealistic hopes of one were widespread. Quite apart from the revolution in weaponry that made life on the battlefields very different from what the generals had been expecting, the Germans could also counterbalance the Entente with allies of their own: initially the Austro-Hungarian empire, and later Turkey.

Within this gigantic conflict it soon became clear that the most advanced and concentrated form of warfare was mainly centred on the 'Western' front in Belgium and northern France. In strategic terms this was the key to the whole of western Europe, while in military terms it was always the decisive theatre. It was the scene of the main German assault in August 1914 and then, when the Germans reverted to the defensive in the West, it remained their centre of gravity. Their main army remained in place there, and was hard pressed to contain repeated large offensives by the two most technologically advanced members of the Entente. If the German gains could not be reversed here, they could not be reversed anywhere.

But why did the war break out at all? Some commentators like to make rather airy and intangible generalizations about the rigid stratification of social classes at the time, combined with a traditional view of war almost as 'the sport of kings'. More credibly, we should recognize the importance of another and harder-edged type of logic, based on realpolitik and the iron necessities of national survival. In particular we can point to the system of opposing alliances by which the European 'balance of power' had been maintained for many decades, but with accelerating intensity since the establishment of the German empire in 1871. By 1907 Britain had joined the Entente Cordiale with France and Russia, as a power bloc facing the 'Central Powers' of Germany and Austro-Hungary. Several different arms races were run between the two sides; not only to build bigger armies and navies, but also in terms of metallurgical and chemical industries, in the building of fortifications and in the acquisition of colonies. Each of these separate arms races had its own pace and dynamic, and could lead to widely different results. For example, a colonial confrontation such as that between Britain and France at Fashoda in 1898, or between France and Germany at Agadir in 1911, could

The Start of the War and of the Western Front

bring tensions to a head and so help to produce a local diplomatic settlement. On the other hand, sabre-rattling might easily have a distinctly destabilizing effect. Most notably, the French law of 7 August 1913 to increase the size of the army by extending the period of conscription to three years led the German General Staff to calculate that it would be advantageous for them to force a show-down with France sooner rather than later. According to this analysis the almost mathematical result was a war that started in August 1914.

Arms races and the confrontations between opposing alliances might often seem to proceed with a sense of inevitability, but we must always remember that at any moment the personal intervention of some imaginative individual might change the underlying logic and break what might appear to be a pre-ordained chain of events. In fact the whole concept of a 'balance' of power should demand that the system is always geared to veer away from a 'total' war whenever it threatens. Limited wars might sometimes be acceptable to achieve a necessary local correction within the overall balance, but these should never be allowed to escalate into a general conflagration. The problem with the start of the Great War was that this mechanism did not work at the critical moments, although we can readily acknowl-edge the possibility that a statesman of vision might have stepped in to keep the confrontation limited.[1]

In 1914 the particular war that ought to have been kept limited was the long-running dispute between Austro-Hungary and Serbia over Bosnia and Herzegovina, which both sides claimed. Serbia was a young country in full expansion, anxious to champion the Slav peoples against the sprawling Austro-Hungarian Empire. That empire, by contrast, regarded the Balkans as its own natural area of influence, and was confident in its military power, especially since it was strengthened by an alliance with Germany. The dispute came to a head following the assassination of the Austrian Archduke Franz Ferdinand and his wife in Sarajevo on 28 June. The Vienna govern-ment felt compelled to mobilize against Serbia and, secure in a promise of unconditional German support ('the blank cheque'), declared war on 28 July. We might consider that this in itself was an

The Great War on the Western Front

overreaction. Yet the world had already seen a series of small Balkan wars in 1912–13, and many outsiders expected that this one would be no bigger. However, on this occasion Russia had already given plentiful warning that she would not stand idly by, but would mobilize in support of her Serbian friends: fellow Slavs whom the Tsar had not been able to help as much as he would have liked during the earlier conflicts. We might criticize this move as a second over-reaction, although when seen from a different perspective it ought perhaps to have served as a salutary deterrent which could have persuaded Austria to stand down and not pursue any war at all. It did indeed shake the Germans out of their complacency, and they belatedly attempted to restrain their Austrian allies, but their inter-vention came too late. The die had already been cast.

Russia was certainly clumsy in the method of her mobilization, which began on 29 July as a partial measure to face Austria alone, then was extended to cover Germany as well, then was reduced back again. However, it was finally extended the next day to cover the whole of her western frontier, including the more northerly portion which faced Germany. This naturally set alarm bells ringing in Berlin, where the General Staff threw its influence behind a call for the maximum mobilization not merely of Austria, but also of Germany herself. The German chancellor Theobold von Bethmann-Hollweg, who wanted a more conciliatory approach, was overruled. Germany finally declared war on Russia on 1 August. Thus a limited war in Serbia was set to expand into a much less limited – albeit also rather less intended – war in western Russia. Even so, this still apparently amounted to considerably less than the prospect of a 'world con-flagration'.

It was unfortunately at this point that Helmuth von Moltke (the younger), chief of the German General Staff, disingenuously insisted that his forces were configured only for a war on two fronts, rather than just one. If only he had been more sympathetic to the diplomats, he might well have been able to find the means to limit German mobilization to the Russian front alone; but he did not. He believed not only that France would definitely give military help to her ally if Russia became involved in any fighting, but also that France posed a

The Start of the War and of the Western Front

much more immediate threat to Germany than did Russia. The French centres of mobilization were closer to Berlin than the Russians', and the French army and defence industries were more modern. Therefore the famous 'Schlieffen Plan', which had moulded German doctrine for nearly two decades, laid it down that any campaign against the Entente had to begin with a pre-emptive strike to destroy the French army first.[2] In fact seven out of the eight German armies were sent to attack in the west, while only one was left to defend against the Russians in the east.

This doctrine determined, in effect, that Germany was unable to contemplate a 'limited' war against Russia alone. France was seen as the major threat, which meant that the war would inevitably spread into western as well as eastern Europe. It would involve not only France herself, but also Belgium and Luxembourg – which the Germans saw as the least well-defended highway to Paris – and Britain which, although many of her citizens may not have known it at the time, was more or less inextricably committed to supporting the Entente. The Liberal prime minister, Herbert Henry Asquith, believed that a successful German invasion of France would represent a cataclysmic disaster for the British Empire, and he played a careful hand to win over his sceptical cabinet to the same point of view. The fact that Germany was violating Belgian neutrality gave him the moral argument that he needed, so his efforts were successful. The final diplomatic efforts to restore peace broke down during the first three days of August. Germany declared war on France on the 3rd, Belgium was entered by German troops during the night of the 3rd to 4th, and the British declared war later on the 4th. The Western Front had been opened, and already it was being seen as the most decisive front of all.

Thus it was that a war that need never have happened, or which might have been contained within the Balkans, or at least no further afield than western Russia, spread almost instantly to embrace a great part of Europe. From there, since Britain, France, Belgium and Germany were among the leading colonial powers at the time, it was but a short step to involving a great deal of the rest of the world, at least in a technical sense. Other colonial powers included Italy,

The Great War on the Western Front

Portugal, Japan and the USA, who all sooner or later joined the Entente; and Holland and Spain, who somehow managed to remain neutral. Japan was keen to pick off the German colonies in the Pacific and joined the war on 23 August, soon exploiting the international situation to occupy a part of China. In general, however, the fighting in non-European areas remained somewhat minor or marginal, with the possible exception of the campaigns in Palestine and Mesopotamia. Even the relatively large 'Eastern' campaign in the Dardanelles in 1915 was still fought technically just within the geographical boundaries of Europe. By contrast, the Second World War would turn out to be far more truly global in its scope, with its most advanced weapons being tested nowhere near Europe, but as far away as Nevada, Hiroshima and Nagasaki.

THE OPENING OF THE WESTERN FRONT

The Western Front was a battlefield that had been carefully prepared in advance. Ever since the war of 1870–1 the Franco-German border had been heavily fortified by the two sides, who recognized that sooner or later a renewal of hostilities would be inevitable. Yet so thoroughly had the French built the defences on their side of the frontier that the Germans began to look for ways to avoid making a direct frontal attack. They selected a more open approach through Luxembourg and south-east Belgium, by which they could outflank their opponent from the north. The Belgians in turn built new fortifications, in Liège, Namur and Antwerp, though at first this did not worry the Germans. For a long time they believed that they could bully or bribe the cynical old Belgian king Leopold II into granting them free passage, although when he died in 1909 his successor Albert I turned out to be made of sterner stuff, and under his leadership the Belgians would resist energetically in 1914.

In the event the Germans were forced to fight their way through Belgium; but by 1914 they had strengthened their spearheads with a new generation of heavy howitzers, which were able to smash even the most modern concrete forts. Liège and Namur fell in short order, and then a second surprise was revealed. A new and wider German

The Start of the War and of the Western Front

mobilization system had allowed them to put some 40 per cent more troops into Belgium than the French intelligence service had predicted. *Der Millionenkrieg* ('the million-man war') had arrived with a vengeance, and would continue to grow and grow in scale for the next four years. Given their unexpectedly great numbers, the Germans did not confine themselves merely to the Ardennes area to the south-east of the country, but swept much more widely to the west, occupying Brussels and even threatening Antwerp. Their main thrust therefore emerged in northern France almost 100 miles nearer to the Channel coast than had been calculated by the French planners.

On their side the French 'Plan XVII' had been based on an expectation that the Germans would always enjoy a numerical superiority, albeit a much smaller one than would actually be the case. They would attempt to encircle each French contingent from the flanks, to which the recommended French antidote was that their outnumbered forces should launch a rapid counter-attack against the enemy's centre or rear, designed to disrupt him and prevent the completion of his encirclement. While the more numerous Germans could afford to make outflanking attacks, therefore, the French would be compelled to make a risky frontal assault as their only alternative to retreat. Many historians have misunderstood the military logic behind this analysis, and have characterized it as merely a blind and even suicidal offensive *à outrance*. It was actually a great deal more subtle than that, and rested not only upon a traditional theme of French military thought that went back at least two centuries, but also upon some of the most modern scientific writing in the field of crowd psychology.[3] The leading theorists of the offensive doctrine, such as de Maud'huy or de Grandmaison, were very far from being the spiritualist idiots they have too often been portrayed as.

Plan XVII called for two major offensives: one, with two armies, directly across the eastern frontier into the German-occupied parts of Alsace and Lorraine; and a second, with another two armies, into the Belgian Ardennes. The first of these attacks was largely a political gesture, since the public demanded pure and unsophisticated revenge for the loss of territory in 1871. But in military terms it was deeply

The Great War on the Western Front

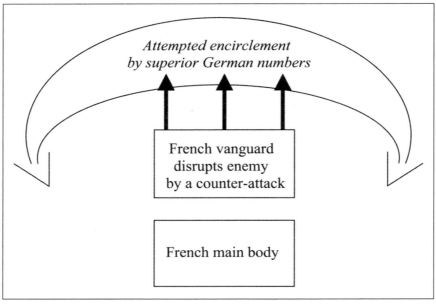

Attempted encirclement
by superior German numbers

French vanguard
disrupts enemy
by a counter-attack

French main body

The French theory of the vanguard. The theoretical French antidote to attempted German encirclements.

foolhardy, since the Germans had enjoyed four decades in which to prepare the battlefields, and sure enough the attacks were defeated and driven back from Morhange and Sarrebourg on 20–22 August. This incident should not, however, be seen as a failure of tactics, but rather of the interaction between strategy, policy and press expectations at the highest level. It is more than unfortunate that the highly political imperatives behind the offensive into Alsace-Lorraine have been hidden in the general rush to shift the blame from the politicians to the generals.

The second offensive was planned on a much more military basis. It was designed to cut in behind the main German spearheads advancing into Belgium and, if it had worked, it would surely have disrupted the Schlieffen Plan very effectively. Unfortunately for the French, however, the fact that the Germans had mobilized many more troops than expected meant that they had a powerful second

The Start of the War and of the Western Front

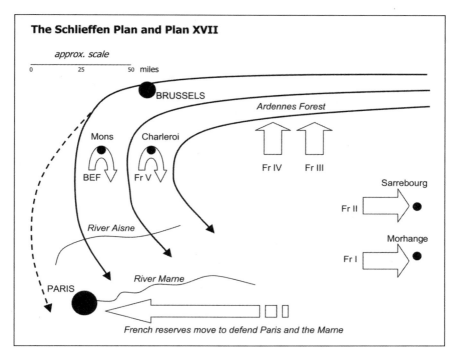

echelon marching into Belgium behind their leading troops, so the assault hit those rather than the soft logistic rear that they had hoped to find. Once again the attackers were dispersed with heavy losses. Meanwhile the German spearheads further to the west were appearing in great strength in front of the fifth French army, which held them up for three days at Charleroi, and a small British army (the British Expeditionary Force, or BEF) that delayed them for twelve hours at Mons. In both cases the final result was the same: the allies began a long retreat to the south in the hot August weather, while the Germans pushed onwards towards Paris at the quickstep.

Nothing that happened after that had been expected by anyone. At the very least the allies had expected an honourable draw in the 'Battles of the Frontiers', instead of which they now had to deal with the reality of a comprehensive defeat. It was only the reassuring imperturbability of the French commander, 'Papa' Joseph Joffre, that

The Great War on the Western Front

held them all together through the crisis. His only previous field command had been at the head of 1,000 troops in Timbuktu in 1894–5, yet now, incongruously, he found himself commanding an army of well over a million men on a frontage of over 400 miles, in the face of the most powerful and professional army in the world. Few in the upper reaches of the French high command had expected him to shine, but during August and September 1914 he did exactly what was necessary to save France, calmly moving reserves by rail from the eastern frontier to the threatened areas around Paris and the Marne river on its eastern flank. Not all of his army commanders did as well. For example, the previously high-flying General Charles Lanrezac, who had commanded at Charleroi, suffered something of a breakdown and was 'sent to Limoges' (Limogé), or in other words fired. The British Field Marshal Sir John French did scarcely better, and only a few days after his first battle was talking about retreating to the Loire and removing his army from France altogether. He had to be 'stiffened up' by a personal visit from the great Field Marshal Horatio Herbert Kitchener, and it is remarkable that he survived in command after that. Thus a considerable proportion of the individuals who had been selected as key commanders before the war failed the test of modern battle.

On the German side exactly the same can be said of von Moltke himself. Soon after the spectacularly successful opening phase of his campaign, he sensed that control of events was gradually slipping away from him. His HQ was located too far behind the spearheads – which were marching at maximum speed away from him – and he discovered, too late, that too much personal initiative had been allowed to each of his seven army commanders. On the Alsace frontier Crown Prince Rupprecht of Bavaria, commanding the sixth army, had been told to retire before the French offensive, to lure them further away from Paris, but instead he counter-attacked, with a diametrically opposite result. Equally the army commanders on the vital western flank edged their line of march successively eastwards, in order to keep in touch with their neighbours, but in so doing they abandoned Schlieffen's essential idea that Paris should be encircled from the west. In the event the main German blow emerged to the

The Start of the War and of the Western Front

east of the French capital, which meant that it could not achieve anything like the decisive victory that had been hoped. At that point it became clear not only that the French defence on the Marne had been consolidated and reinforced, but that the leading German troops had lost cohesion and were exhausted by their long march in the heat. On 9 September they were abruptly pulled back to more defensible lines some forty miles further north, while von Moltke himself suffered a breakdown and had to be replaced, by General Erich von Falkenhayn. Joffre thus enjoyed the satisfaction of victory in 'the battle of the Marne', although he was left with the deeply intractable problem that the Germans still occupied a deep and wide swathe of northern France and, even worse, had adopted a particularly well-organized defensive posture.

In the allied 'pursuit' northwards from the Marne the underlying strength of the defensive in modern warfare began to become apparent in a way that had not previously been understood. On the heights above the Aisne (the Chemin des Dames), for example, the Germans were able to beat off every attack. Then in the Ypres salient the British in turn, under General Sir Douglas Haig, were able to hold their positions against fierce counter-attacks, including the notorious 'Kindermord' in which regiments of inexpert young Germans rushed forward near Langemarck only to be mown down in their hundreds. Both sides attempted to stake claims and outflank their opponents, only to find that they soon ran out of flanks. At its extreme western end the line rested on the North Sea. South-east of Ypres the Germans held the Lille industrial area and Vimy Ridge, while the allies held Arras and Albert. The line continued to drive roughly south-south-east to Noyon, which formed the point of a salient in German hands, then it veered sharply eastwards along the Chemin des Dames. Reims was held by the French, as was the fortress complex around Verdun, although the Germans had cut in further south with a sharp salient around St Mihiel. From there the line regained roughly the pre-war frontier, west of the German fortress of Metz, and so down 'the blue line of the Vosges' to the Swiss border. By mid-November the front had solidified along its whole length, and four long and frustrating years of 'trenchlock' had begun. This would almost immediately

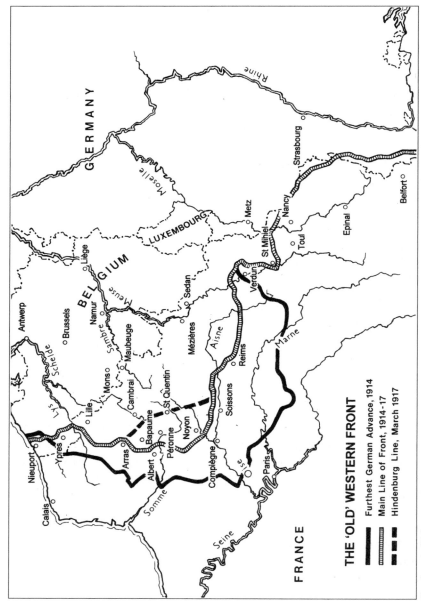

THE 'OLD' WESTERN FRONT

Furthest German Advance, 1914
Main Line of Front, 1914-17
Hindenburg Line, March 1917

Map drawn by Ed Dovey.

14

The Start of the War and of the Western Front

become the most notoriously memorable feature of the Western Front, and the source of all the frustrations and heavy casualties that are associated with it.

There were three main elements in the new power of the defence. The first was the extensive use of fortifications such as barbed wire entanglements, multiple lines of trenches and bombproof dugouts. Secondly, there were the light weapons of the front-line troops; not only the rifles and machine guns that had been well known before the war, but a whole new generation of weapons that were designed during the winter of 1914–15 specifically to meet the novel requirements of trench combat. These included many different types of hand grenade, trench mortar and trench cannon, and flamethrowers would be added to the list by 1916. Last but far from least was the artillery that supported the front line, firing from relatively safe positions in the rear. It could bring down an unprecedentedly heavy volume of fire upon 'no man's land' and the enemy's trenches that lay beyond it, but during at least the first three years of the war it was itself very difficult to hit.

It is the machine gun that has captured the popular imagination as the great killing machine of this war, since it was not only a 'machine' but also an inhuman or 'nerveless' weapon when used on fixed lines with awesomely 'automatic' fire. It did not need to be aimed personally, like a rifle or grenade, but seemed to take on almost a life of its own. At certain moments it could dominate the battlefield for a mile around its firing point, allowing just a handful of its servants to mow down whole lines of soldiers in the space of a very few minutes. Such moments, however, were rare. For most of the rest of the war the great majority of casualties (estimated as about 60 per cent) were caused by artillery, especially with High Explosive (HE) ammunition. HE had been invented in the 1880s, when almost overnight it was found that the great explosive power that could be packed into each shell had made most existing fortifications obsolete. In future any trench or masonry wall would be very vulnerable, so the choice facing defenders was between excavating dugouts much deeper into the ground (say twenty feet), or screening themselves with thick layers of reinforced concrete. Then there was a second technical revolution in artillery around 1900, when efficient hydraulic systems were developed which absorbed the recoil of each shot without transmitting it to the trail or wheels, so that the gun did not move and have to be relaid every time. This in turn allowed a vastly increased rate of accurate fire to be delivered on any chosen target, with perhaps up to fifteen or, with the famous French 75mm field gun, even twenty-five shots per minute.

All this was widely known by the European armies at an intellectual level, but it was only in real large-scale combat that the various different innovations, and the way they interacted with each other, came to be understood at a deeper and more instinctive level. The learning process could often be slow. For one thing, many of the field gunners suddenly had to learn the scientific art of indirect fire at long range (that is, when the target was not visible to the gunners), and their pre-war training had become obsolete, concentrating almost exclusively on direct fire at relatively close range, and on horse care, without which the guns would have been immobile. Then again, both the optimum use of machine guns, and the counter-measures against them, took a surprisingly long time for the infantry to work out. It was only about halfway through the war that basic platoon tactics for the attack were properly mastered by the British – somewhat later than they were by the French, and somewhat earlier than by the Germans.

CHAPTER TWO

Late 1914 and the Battles of 1915: Birth of a New Style of Warfare

Late 1914 and the Battles of 1915

The Western Front was built mostly by French, German and Belgian armies that were based on universal short-service conscription, backed up by lengthy reserve commitments. In other words, almost the entire male population had to serve with the colours for a time before reverting to civilian life, but still remaining liable to be called back in the event of a national crisis. This meant that the whole population was trained for war and more or less ready to fight. In Britain, by contrast, the peacetime army was volunteer, all-regular and long-service. This meant that it was small, drawn from a relatively small proportion of the population, and normally having little contact with the rest. It was designed for routine colonial policing rather than for a one-off 'Great War', which meant that when Britain found herself involved in such an unexpected event, exceptional measures had to be taken. What happened was that Kitchener and Lord Derby called for millions of 'hostilities only' volunteers who would be neither conscripts nor regulars. They did indeed join up in vast numbers in 1914, providing the manpower for many 'New Army' divisions. The problem was that there was little by way of infrastructure prepared to receive them, so they often had to waste many months before they could be properly equipped and trained. In fact it would not be until 1916 that most of the New Army divisions could take the field, and 1 July of that year turned out to be the fatal date on which many of them suffered their baptism of fire. In the meantime, through 1914, 1915 and the first half of 1916 it was the French army that had to bear the main brunt of the allied war on the Western Front.

The problem for the French was that they were forced to go on the offensive, because the Germans were now diverting reserves to the Eastern Front, against Russia, while adopting a largely defensive posture inside Belgium and France. In political terms it was not an option to simply leave them in place, although in military terms it would be very difficult to push them back. From the British perspective these difficulties soon raised major strategic questions, since there were many who still doubted the wisdom of deploying a large

The Great War on the Western Front

army to France at all. This became a debate between the 'Westerners', mainly in the army but largely supported by Prime Minister Asquith, who believed that the Western Front was the decisive theatre and should always be given priority, and the 'Easterners', who wanted to find an easier path by going round the flanks. Churchill and Lloyd George would become the leading lights in the latter movement, not least because they wanted to set out a position that was different from Asquith's. Their first blow fell on the Dardanelles on 19 February 1915, leading on to a hopeless campaign that would last eleven long months. Churchill himself was removed from the Admiralty as early as May, when Asquith widened his Liberal government into a coalition with the Conservative opposition.

Meanwhile on the Western Front there were few signs of a reliable method for making a breakthrough. In the Battle of the Frontiers the French army had already discovered that it was badly deficient in heavy and even medium artillery, and that the standard of co-operation between the gunners and the foot soldiers left much to be desired. Communications between artillery and infantry were notoriously difficult in the days before the radio became common-place, especially for an attacker who had to readjust fire at frequent intervals to keep up with a rapidly changing situation. Joffre issued a stream of directives attempting to improve these tactics, and he ruthlessly weeded out incompetent commanders wherever he thought he detected them. The task, however, was too big and too intractable even for him. In essence a whole new 'art of war' had to be invented almost from scratch, and it would take a long time and hundreds of thousands of casualties before that could be achieved.

After the front had been established by November 1914, Joffre began a new series of attacks as early as 20 December, attempting to pinch out the flanks of what was known as the 'Noyon salient', in Artois and Champagne respectively. They were known as 'nibbling' (or in French 'grignotage') attacks, which implied a type of attrition in which gradual progress would nevertheless be made, but unfortunately they were sent in piecemeal over too wide a frontage and on too small a scale. There were a few gains in eastern Champagne, but in general the whole offensive was a complete failure, and it sputtered

Late 1914 and the Battles of 1915

out on 17 March 1915. Meanwhile some fierce mountaintop battles flared in the Vosges, again bringing no success to the French.

One of the more encouraging episodes was at Neuve Chapelle in Artois on 10–13 March, when the British attacked on a two-mile front behind a particularly well-concentrated artillery bombardment. This was initially very successful, and suggested that a mathematical relationship could be established between the number of shells fired per mile of front, and the speed of the advance. It was doubly worrying to the Germans because they had only a single line of trenches, and this had been overrun. They nevertheless demonstrated characteristic tactical flexibility by bringing up sufficient reserves to plug the gap with an improvised second line of defence, and this was effective. The British found that their initial bombardment had used up most of their available ammunition in the space of a few minutes (15 per cent of the total British stocks in France), and attempts to renew the assault could make no further progress.

The Battle of Neuve Chapelle pointed lessons for the future to both sides. The British saw how powerful properly concentrated artillery could be, and how it might be used to achieve a breakthrough. However, in their next two attacks, at Aubers Ridge on 9 May and Festubert on 15 May, they were too short of guns and ammunition to be able to repeat the fleeting success of 10 March. For their part, the Germans were motivated to build second and even third lines of defence all along the front. By 1917 their concept of 'defence in depth' would be elaborated with very great sophistication, constantly multiplying the difficulties facing an attacker in proportion as the attackers devised new techniques of their own.

Perhaps the most dramatic of all the new assault techniques unveiled in this war was poison gas (chlorine), which the Germans finally used on 22 April 1915 at the second battle of Ypres. They had wanted to use it much earlier, essentially as an experiment, but the launch had been delayed for some time by contrary winds. When it eventually came, it happened to land on a remarkably wide selection of allied nationalities – Belgians, Algerians, French, British and Canadians – and it had a devastating effect on most of them. The Canadians held out most stoutly, but even so a four-mile-wide gap was opened, through which the Germans might have advanced past them into central Ypres. In the event they failed to seize their chance, whether from fear of their own gas or from sheer disbelief that a breakthrough had actually been achieved. Whatever the reason, the moment passed and the allies were able to consolidate a line, albeit considerably further to the rear than they had started. Bitter fighting continued until 25 May, including some new German gas attacks, but the chance of a breakthrough never recurred. Apart from anything else, the allies proved to be faster in adopting relatively good anti-gas measures than their opponents had expected.

Meanwhile the French launched a new offensive against Vimy Ridge in Artois on 9–15 May, with a brief renewal on 15–19 June. General Philippe Pétain achieved a dramatic initial success in the centre, but overall this battle, like so many others, was marked mainly by frustration and heavy casualties in the face of defences that the attacker had no means of capturing. There was, nevertheless, one pregnant pointer for the future hidden in the midst of Pétain's attack, when a Captain André Laffargue achieved a local tactical success with his platoon near Neuville St Vaast on 9 May. He analyzed the lessons in a pamphlet that soon became very influential not only in the French army, but among the British and German forces as well. What he was saying was basically that infantry armed with a selection of the new trench weapons could hope to achieve success on their own, without having to wait for artillery support to catch up. His formula depended firstly on each platoon or company developing as much firepower as possible with its own rifles, grenades, machine guns, mortars and trench cannons. But secondly he stressed the need to press forward into whatever gaps could be found in the enemy line or, in other words, to use 'infiltration' or 'stormtroop' tactics. Laffargue's ideas would reverberate for the remainder of the war among all armies, and in essence they represented the blueprint for infantry tactics throughout the rest of the twentieth century. In modern literature it is often alleged that it was the Germans who invented stormtroop tactics, since they used them to particularly good effect in the spring offensives of 1918; in fact they date back to

Late 1914 and the Battles of 1915

the French as early as May 1915, and the British formally incorporated them in a manual issued in February 1917.

When taken together, the novel British techniques with artillery at Neuve Chapelle, the German use of gas at Second Ypres, and the French pioneering of stormtroop tactics on Vimy Ridge, all pointed to different aspects of the future of warfare. At the time, however, none of them stood out as clear 'revolutions', but remained submerged within wider battles that all ended in frustration and heavy casualties. The same can be said of the much older 'breakthrough technology' of mine tunnelling. Many mines were dug during 1915 and 1916, notably at St Eloi, Hill 60 at Ypres and perhaps most significantly at Messines, where a particularly elaborate array of mines was dug in 1916 but not blown until 7 June 1917. With charges of HE rather than gunpowder all these mines promised to yield a much bigger effect than had been possible in the days of Vauban or Guy Fawkes. Yet they were no easier or less perilous to dig than they had been in the past, and they required specialist diggers: usually men who had been coal miners in civilian life. Nor can it be said that they really changed the course of battles. It was notoriously difficult to co-ordinate the explosion of the mine with the infantry attack needed to capture the enemy position that it destroyed. Often the attacking troops would be just as shocked by the power of the explosion as the defenders, and in any case not even the biggest mine could have any more than a somewhat localized effect. It was only at Messines in 1917 that a large number of large mines – nineteen in all, containing a total of almost a million pounds of explosive – was detonated simultaneously, to wipe out the entire German front line. Even then, however, it was only the front line that was captured. In later battles the slow and laborious process of mining would be abandoned in favour of faster and more easily repeatable methods, such as the tank.

The tank was a marriage of armour plate with caterpillar tracks driven by an internal combustion engine. It had been a theoretical possibility for many years and had even captured the popular imagination, most notably in H.G. Wells's short story 'The Land Ironclads', which appeared in 1903.[1] Yet in the technological conditions of 1915 such a machine was extraordinarily difficult to design and build, and most military authorities were sceptical that it could be done at all, or even that it was worth doing. Little would have happened unless Winston Churchill, the First Lord of the Admiralty, had thrown his quirky personal brand of energy behind it. Presumably he saw the creation of a 'battleship' for trench warfare as a naval responsibility, even though no one in the army had asked him to do it. Even so, tanks would not be seen in battle until September 1916, and would not make a major impact until November 1917.

Another new technology that had a much greater, and earlier, impact than the tank was the aeroplane. Already during the mobile operations of August 1914 it had performed some excellent reconnaissance work, showing that it could search far faster and deeper into unknown enemy territory than traditional cavalry. Then, as the fighting became more static, the value of aerial observation for artillery spotting was quickly appreciated as the key to accurate long-range fire, although it would be more than a year before ways were found to arm aircraft effectively for dog-fighting. Recognizable fighter planes became available in significant numbers only over the winter of 1915–16, when it was the Germans who took the lead, most notably with their Fokker Eindekker series. In that period a total of some 300 of these machines were able to shoot down about 1,000 enemy aircraft, before the aerial balance of power on the Western Front swung completely back to the allies.

Meanwhile many experiments were being made by both sides to conduct 'strategic bombing'. There were allied raids to destroy German Zeppelin sheds from September 1914 onwards, whereas the Zeppelins were themselves soon being used to bomb cities such as Antwerp in August 1914 and London in January 1915. Both sides then hastened to design heavy fixed-wing bombers for this role, with the British Handley Page series being the heaviest and most numerous, but the German Gothas making a particularly noticeable impact on London in 1917.

It would be several years after the outbreak of war before either tanks or aircraft would be able to make a truly important impact on the ground battle. In the meantime defenders in general still retained

Late 1914 and the Battles of 1915

the advantage over attackers by a very wide margin, and the profile of every battle remained depressingly uniform. The attacker might make some dramatic initial gains by some innovative artifice or 'secret weapon', but he would quickly get bogged down as the impetus slipped away and the defender brought his artillery and reserves to bear with murderous effect.

This pattern continued on 25 September 1915, when Joffre launched large-scale attacks in the eastern Champagne, as well as in Artois, once again on either side of the Noyon salient. In Artois the French attack on Vimy Ridge was co-ordinated with a British attack at nearby Loos, although it did not prosper. In the Champagne the maximum French advance was about two miles, but momentum was soon lost and the offensive had petered out by 6 October. The Germans regained most of the lost ground by counter-attacks, especially a large and carefully prepared one on 30 October. At Loos the story was somewhat similar. The British used gas for the first time, in part to compensate for the inadequate scale of their artillery support. However, the timing of the attack was not flexible, since it had to fit in with Joffre's wider timetable, which meant that the gas was released before the wind was strong enough to carry it into the German lines. It hung in no man's land, and in places wafted back into the British trenches, causing numerous friendly casualties. Nevertheless at some parts of the line the attack did drive straight through the German front line in fine style, only to be held up further back and then repulsed by counter-attacks. The British had not yet perfected the very difficult techniques needed to consolidate a captured position rapidly, or to direct reinforcements to the points where they were most needed. At Loos this last point generated an acrimonious controversy, in the course of which two inexperienced 'New Army' divisions and their commanders were shamefully scapegoated for Sir John French's mistakes. This provoked Haig to exploit his privileged access to the King, in order to blacken French's name. Finally, on 10 December 1915, less than a week after Lloyd George had displaced Asquith as prime minister, Haig's intrigues won him the ultimate success, and he displaced French as commander-in-chief of the BEF.

The Great War on the Western Front

In the days before tactical radio there was no easy way for a commander to get timely news of what had happened at the front, so that he could make best use of his reserves. In particular it was not possible to lay survivable telephone cables across no man's land during the short time an attack was still in progress. Unless such cables were carefully buried some six feet below ground level, they were very likely to be severed by shell fire. There was thus a crucial 'communications gap' between the trenches from which the attackers jumped off, and the first enemy trench that they might capture. More than any other factor, perhaps, this did much to ensure the continuing superiority of the defensive over the offensive. There would thus be no breakthrough in 1915, although the prospect of one always continued to tantalize tacticians.

Without any dramatic movement of the fronts, the troops were forced to get used to an extremely static and uncomfortable style of warfare. In the face of random shelling or mortaring they had to learn to dig much deeper into the earth than their pre-war manuals had ever imagined. Against random sniping they had to crouch low below the parapets of their trenches, which were often less than five feet high, and certainly lower than the ideal recommended by engineering theory. Against rain and snow they had to use whatever shelter they could find, which was usually very inadequate, as were the arrangements for draining water away from the muddy floors of the trenches. The troops would often be left cold, soaked through and exposed to a variety of diseases, not least 'trench foot'. Above all, however, they had to learn to make do without sleep. By night they had to patrol no man's land or improve the wire entanglements in front of their trenches; by day they had to dig those trenches deeper.

In these circumstances it soon became obvious that no troops could be expected to remain in the front line for very many days at a time. They burned up too quickly, even when enemy action was minimal. A complex system of reliefs was therefore set up whereby each brigade would begin well to the rear of the fighting lines, supposedly resting in comfortable billets and far from the risk of shelling. Then after a

Late 1914 and the Battles of 1915

few days it would move up into the second line, where long-range enemy fire might reach it, and where the men would find plenty of support, logistical and engineering tasks to occupy their time. After a few more days they would relieve the men in the very front line, and take on full combat responsibilities for a time. But then they would be sent back to the second line once again, and so the 'Jacob's Ladder' of reliefs would continue. In theory it was an ideal system, and even humane. In practice it was far from that, since every relief involved complex movements at night, as the fresh troops stumbled up dark communications trenches to occupy unfamiliar fighting positions, while the spent troops stumbled back to rearward lines where, instead of being allowed to 'rest', they would find that the demands upon them only multiplied. Even more digging or handling of stores would be required, although at least the threat of death by enemy fire would be less. In 1915–16 there were very few weapons with an effective range that extended very much further than the opposing second defensive line, so troops who had been pulled back behind that were usually safe. But by 1917 this would change, as a result of increased aerial bombardment and more accurate long-range artillery.

In the front line there was never any assured safety, even on 'quiet' sections of the front, or at slack times when no great offensives were in the offing. Even when there was no obvious need for it, certain commanding officers and certain whole units liked to cultivate a reputation for being particularly thrusting, hyperactive or élite. Even when there was a notorious shortage of shells, as there was for all armies throughout much of 1915, certain artillery units liked to fire off their allocation as quickly as possible, and then cry for more. In some units remorseless trench raiding and aggressive patrolling in no man's land became elevated into a source of pride and almost a cult. All of these things inevitably made life exceptionally dangerous for whatever enemy unit was unfortunate enough to find itself manning the trenches opposite to the 'thrusters', since they would be harassed constantly and would suffer significantly higher casualties than might normally be expected. They would, in short, be forced to fight back rather than being allowed to serve out their time in the trenches in a state of passive inaction.

On the other hand, a significantly different situation obtained in the many sections of the Western Front where no such 'thrusters' were present. Especially during the shell shortage, many front line units discovered that if they did not provoke the enemy infantry opposite them, the enemy artillery would not fire back. In this and many other ways it was often possible to reduce casualties by what Tony Ashworth has called 'the live and let live system':[2] the observation of informal or tacit mutual ceasefires between the two sides.

The best-known example was the 'Christmas truce' of 1914, which included such non-bellicose behaviour as carol singing across the lines and an impromptu football match between British and German soldiers.[3] The high commands on both sides were scandalized, and cracked down on such overt fraternization, but what they could not do was ensure that their men always displayed maximum aggression. Troops in the front line were acutely aware that if they went out of their way to fire at the enemy whenever possible, or to patrol no man's land energetically, the enemy would surely retaliate in kind. Everyone's casualties would rise which, if there was no offensive in progress and no sensible tactical objective to be captured, would amount to a particularly purposeless sacrifice. On large sections of the Western Front for much of the time, therefore, the soldiers simply kept their heads down and tried to avoid attracting enemy retaliation. Sometimes they were compelled to open fire to satisfy the demands of higher commanders, but they would often find ways to do it at times and places designed to cause minimum damage, or in predictable ways that would allow the enemy to keep out of harm's way in due turn. Thus it was that some parts of this notoriously 'dangerous' theatre of war could remain almost entirely inactive for months at a time. For example, there was one British battalion that served honourably in or near the front line for an entire year, suffering only one officer casualty.[4] This experience was very far from the oft-quoted notion that the average life expectancy of subalterns on the Western Front was no more than three weeks.

Late 1914 and the Battles of 1915

Of course, none of this reflects on the levels of casualties habitually suffered in major offensives, which were almost always shockingly high. The British lost over 90,000 in their four relatively small offensives from Neuve Chapelle to Loos, quite apart from the daily attrition of trench life. Bad as this was, it paled into insignificance beside the sacrifices of the French. By the end of 1915 they had already had as many as two million casualties, of whom about a third were killed.

As 1915 dragged on, the news gradually seeped back to the civilian populations at home that the war was no longer being fought at the quickstep, as at least two centuries of military history had led most of the press to expect. Instead, the Western Front had become a gigantic siege, reminiscent of Sevastopol in the 1850s or Petersburg in the 1860s, but all on a massively greater scale, with much more modern weapons and hugely heavier casualties. During the first months of the war the local newspapers had celebrated and highlighted every volunteer who joined up, and individually mourned each one who fell. After a year of war, by contrast, this patriotic enthusiasm had subtly changed into a broader type of coverage. The sheer number of casualties meant not only that it was impractical to write a personal story about each one, but also that casualties were no longer the sort of 'news' that people liked to read. The public had come to realize that military service was actually a great deal more dangerous than had originally been portrayed, and it was becoming increasingly difficult to find young men who would willingly step forward to join the fighting line.

In political terms this translated into a growing desire to find ways to outflank the Western Front, and find alternative theatres where victory would be easier. The Germans were already making their major offensive effort against Russia, and were starting to think seriously about declaring unrestricted submarine warfare. They were warned off for the time being, however, by the outraged US reaction to their sinking of the liner *Lusitania* on 7 May 1915 with the loss of 1,198 lives including 124 Americans. As for the French, they were naturally committed very centrally to the liberation of their national soil in northern and eastern France, although they also maintained

The Great War on the Western Front

their Mediterranean interests with a large fleet and a willingness to send troops to assist allied operations. This theatre had already become significant when Austria first attacked Serbia and started a new Balkan war; it became doubly active when Turkey entered the war against the allies on 29 October 1914, and then Italy joined on the allied side on 23 May 1915.

More than any of the other belligerents it was Britain that tended to look beyond the Western Front to the wider world. Before the war she had been a naval and colonial power with only a laughably small army for continental operations, even though that army now knew that if it allowed Paris to fall, the whole war would be lost. Naval opinion, however, had long been sceptical about the importance of fighting on the Western Front at all. In 1911 'the British way of war' had been described by Sir Julian Corbett as a system of limited campaigns in distant places that could be isolated by superior sea power.[5] In 1914 that doctrine had initially suggested attacks on the Kaiser's naval bases in north-west Germany, or even an amphibious expedition into the Baltic to capture Berlin from the north. However, upon closer analysis neither of these plans was found to be realistic, most notably because of the dense barriers of mines that would have to be crossed, so other possibilities were sought.

The Japanese were already dealing with German colonies in the Pacific, and a large force was being assembled to occupy German South West Africa and East Africa, although it would find a remarkable opponent in Colonel Paul von Lettow-Vorbeck, who would maintain guerrilla action throughout southern Africa until the end of the war, pinning down up to a third of a million British and Dominion troops. No less frustrating was the war against Turkey. A campaign was begun to secure the oilfields of southern Iraq and it started well, although by April 1916 it would end in the disastrous siege of Kut al Amara. Plans were made to invade Palestine from Egypt, but in early 1915 a much more promising idea seemed to be an attempt to force the passage of the Dardanelles. This would permit the capture of Constantinople and the opening of a warm-water sea route to Russia, so that munitions could flow to the Tsar and his beleaguered armies.

Late 1914 and the Battles of 1915

It was Winston Churchill, the First Sea Lord, who was the prime mover of this plan. An Anglo-French naval force was sent in February and March 1915, but failed to make progress against strong Turkish defences. There was a hasty rethink, and an ill-organized Anglo-French (and ANZAC) force of ground troops was eventually landed on the Gallipoli peninsula on 25 April, only to be pinned down in small beachheads from which no further progress could be made. There followed a process of 'reinforcing failure' until a total of almost half a million men had been landed, of whom almost 50 per cent became casualties. The final evacuation took place on 9 January 1916, and Churchill's military reputation lay in ruins for the remainder of the war. This experience doubtless explains why he would be so stridently and unfairly critical of the army and its generals throughout all the rest of his troubled life.

CHAPTER THREE

The Battle of Verdun, 1916

The Battle of Verdun, 1916

VON FALKENHAYN'S ASSAULT

As 1915 drew to its close, the Western allies seemed to be no closer to breaking the German defences of the Western Front by frontal assault, nor to outflanking them at places like Gallipoli. Very major advances had been made in the theoretical science of trench warfare; but practical applications dragged sadly far behind. The total mobilization of industry remained incomplete, and the after-effects of the shell shortages would linger long into 1916. In France the production of heavy artillery was only just starting to come on stream, while in Britain the Kitchener armies of hostilities-only volunteers were only half complete. When they arrived at the front they found inhospitable trenches in the depths of winter, as well as a strenuous policy throughout the BEF of trench raiding and patrolling, in order to 'blood' the inexperienced new troops. This was deeply unpopular, since it often seemed to put the men in greatly increased danger for no good tactical purpose; yet from the perspective of the high command it was a necessary reassurance that these unusual soldiers really would fight. Throughout history senior regular officers have always been very suspicious of citizen militias, especially when their training programmes have been improvised on a large scale at short notice.

Despite their widespread unpopularity, repeated trench raids did at least establish a body of expertise for small-unit infantry tactics using the new generation of weaponry. Hand grenades (or 'bombs') were especially in evidence in this type of fighting, which spurred the creation of specialized bombing units and schools. Close and accurate artillery support was also much practised and studied, as were personal camouflage, face-painting and the use of soft-soled footwear. Perhaps more surprisingly, the truly vital importance of careful planning came to be understood. This included full-scale 'dress rehearsals' on mock-ups of the battlefield: a lesson that would eventually be passed back to the generals running much larger operations during the later phases of the Somme in 1916. It was only unfortunate that they had not already understood it during the earlier phases.

The plan for the spring was to use large sections of the Kitchener armies in the first really big British offensive, which they would share with equally large sections of the French army on the Somme sector, on either side of Albert, and almost as far south as Amiens. This plan was disrupted, however, when the Germans unexpectedly launched an offensive of their own on 21 February, against the French fortress of Verdun. In less than a week they had wrong-footed Joffre and made rapid early advances, drawing in major French formations from other sectors of the front.

Von Falkenhayn's sinister purpose at Verdun was to 'bleed the French army white', as he grimly expressed it: he was deliberately accelerating the pace of attrition. By early 1916 it was obvious to everyone that attrition had become a central feature of the war, even though tacticians still dreamed of breakthroughs, decisive victories and mobile operations. Yet attrition could come in two different forms. On one side there was an ancient military idea that one could 'wear out' an enemy by forcing him to deploy and keep a large army in the field, but always refusing battle when matters threatened to come to a head. This had been the successful policy of Fabius Cunctator to negate the tactical genius of Hannibal, or of Maria Theresa's armies against Frederick the Great. In German this technique was called *Ermattungsstrategie*. By contrast, what von Falkenhayn was now embracing was an attempt to 'grind down' the enemy by *Zermerbungskrieg* or, in brutal terms, to kill more of his men than he could stand. This idea, which seemed scientifically innovative in one perspective but horribly primitive in another, depended upon the Germans being able to maintain a favourable 'rate of exchange' with the French in terms of casualties given and received.

In the battles of 1914–15 the French had normally been the attackers and had lost many more men than the Germans which, according to conventional wisdom, was exactly what an attacker had to expect. In German eyes, however, this result had less to do with their defensive posture than with their superior weapons, tactics and general military culture. It did not seem to them that an attacker was necessarily doomed to lose more than a defender, even though the great Schlieffen had worked on that assumption and had tried to make outflanking or encircling movements rather than frontal assaults. The first few days at Verdun seemed to demonstrate that it

The Battle of Verdun, 1916

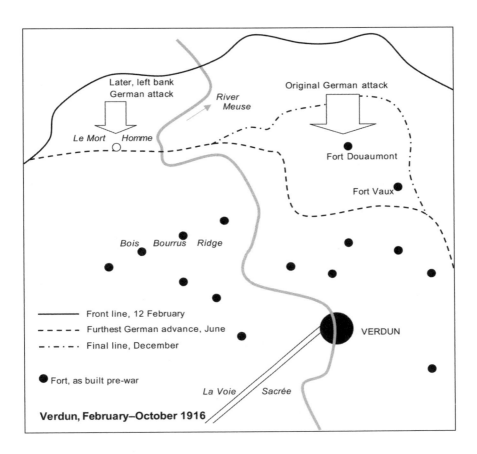

Later, left bank
German attack

Original German attack

River
Meuse

Le Mort   Homme

Fort Douaumont

Fort Vaux

Bois   Bourrus   Ridge

———— Front line, 12 February

– – – – Furthest German advance, June

– · – · – · Final line, December

● Fort, as built pre-war

VERDUN

La Voie   Sacrée

Verdun, February–October 1916

was indeed possible for an attacker to prosper, if he enjoyed superior weapons and tactics as well as the benefits of surprise.

On the other hand von Falkenhayn could scarcely have chosen a more formidable target than Verdun, which was one of the most advanced fortress complexes in the world at the time. In common with Ypres on the allied side and St Mihiel on the German, it was a salient and a bastion that had held out heroically during the phase of mobile war in 1914, thereby shaping the whole layout of the Western Front for the next four years. Together with Arras and Reims it was also a significant city close to the front line that remained in

The Great War on the Western Front

French hands. It therefore held a great symbolic importance that von Falkenhayn well understood. It was politically unthinkable for the French to lose Verdun, so the Germans knew that it would certainly be reinforced heavily if threatened, and that the French army would come crowding into the killing ground that had been chosen for it.

The Germans were also confident that they had sufficient weapons and tactics to do the job. In the first place they still had the super-heavy artillery train that had broken so many modern fortresses in August 1914. Admittedly it was now suffering from worn barrels which reduced accuracy, but it could still deliver 210mm, 305mm and 420mm shells (or 8.25 inch, 12 inch and 16.5 inch respectively). These proved ineffective against a select few of the Verdun forts; but against the rest they were as deadly in 1916 as they had been in Belgium in 1914.

At a lower level, a few German assault pioneers had been trained in 'stormtroop tactics'[1] with a full range of trench weapons, now for the first time including flamethrowers. Their initial impact was strong enough, especially when co-ordinated with a mainly successful plan to achieve surprise, and an unprecedentedly heavy hurricane bombardment. During the first three days the French front line was overrun and suffered very heavy losses; yet the German follow-through was not pressed with adequate urgency or reserves. Even so, one forward patrol was allowed to saunter almost unopposed into the mighty Fort Douaumont on 25 February. Douaumont was a crucial point in the French defensive layout, and its apparently effort-less capture has often been taken as proof that 'German stormtroop tactics' were already decisive in early 1916. In fact this is misleading, since it would be two more years before they became either a wide-spread or a reliable method of advancing speedily against opposition. And then again, it must be said that Douaumont had been stripped of most of its garrison and armament during the previous twelve months. It had been felt that a fortress over three miles behind the front line would never be called upon to defend itself.

The French would suffer enormous casualties before they finally recaptured Douaumont on 24 October, to the extent that it became hallowed ground, symbolizing the whole sacrifice of Verdun, and

The Battle of Verdun, 1916

indeed of the entire war. In the 1920s a gigantic ossuary and cemetery was built nearby as a focus of national remembrance and pilgrimage, equivalent to the Menin Gate and Tyne Cot cemetery at Ypres for the British. Yet perhaps the more important fact was that after they had captured Douaumont on the fourth day of their offensive, it took the Germans four whole months to advance a further two miles; nor did it greatly help them to expand their attack front to the west bank of the Meuse from 6 March. The French consolidated their positions and called in reinforcements. General Pétain took over command, eventually to be hailed as Verdun's saviour. Of particular note was the heroic defence of Fort Vaux, the next serious fort behind Douaumont, which, although it was smaller, put up a great deal more resistance. At Vaux an isolated garrison held out for almost a week, causing some twenty-seven times as many casualties as it suffered, and in the process inspiring a certain Corporal André Maginot to design a whole new post-war generation of fortifications along the Franco-German frontier.

Another pointer to the future was the Voie Sacrée, the 'sacred road' by which the French were supplied. Because Verdun was a salient commanded by German guns on three sides it meant that, apart from one light railway, all the logistics required by her garrison were channelled up a single road. This meant that the maximum possible use had to be made of it, which in turn meant collecting a previously unheard of number of motor lorries, since horsed transport would not be adequate. The trucks would move bumper to bumper in a never-ending crocodile up to the city, alongside a second crocodile coming back. Thousands of men worked night and day to keep the road repaired against the weather and enemy shelling. Altogether it was not only a major achievement of logistics and engineering, but it marked an important milestone in the application of the internal combustion engine to warfare.

The Germans yet again raised the ante on 22 June by introducing a new type of poison gas into the mixture of horror around Verdun: phosgene (or 'Green Cross'). It could defeat the French gas masks of the time, although that particular advantage would soon be eliminated by the introduction of improved masks. The Germans had also perfected the technology of firing gas in artillery shells, rather than simply releasing it from cylinders in the hope that the wind would carry it to the intended target. This was a much more effective way of delivering gas, especially to silence the enemy's artillery lines. Since none of the armies on the Western Front had yet perfected the science of delivering really accurate long-range fire against the enemy's gun batteries, an indiscriminate area weapon like gas made an ideal stop-gap until they did.

THE FRENCH COUNTER-ATTACK

Despite their local surprise with phosgene gas, the Germans' renewed attack soon lost impetus. Joffre intervened to stiffen Pétain's resolve, and it became clear that the French had steadfastly refused to give way. There would be no pushover at Verdun, and General Robert Nivelle's ringing phrase 'Ils ne passeront pas' (They shall not pass) entered the international consciousness. For their part the Germans were soon having to divert resources to both the Eastern Front, where General Alexei Brusilov's Russian offensive was achieving a runaway success, and to the Somme, where Haig's great push was imminent. When von Falkenhayn attempted to revive his attacks on Verdun in early July, he found he could make little headway. By that time he was starting to recognize that his offensive had finally run out of steam, and he was soon forced to revert to the defensive. Thus the Verdun operation, which had started more brilliantly than any seen in 1915 (with the possible exception of the German gas attack at Second Ypres), finally ended no more decisively than any of its predecessors. There can be no doubt that it did indeed become the 'grinding down' battle that von Falkenhayn had planned; but it soon became clear that the Germans were grinding themselves down almost as much as they were grinding down the French.

In most estimates of the battle as a whole the French continued to lose rather more casualties than their opponents, and particularly while they remained on the defensive. There was thus some evidence to corroborate the idea that, given strong artillery, an attacker could now lose fewer men than a defender. However, it was never a

The Battle of Verdun, 1916

dramatically big difference. After the first few days the attacking Germans did not enjoy any decisive advantage in terms of relative attrition. By the end of the battle in late December, each side is thought to have suffered something like 350,000 casualties, of which perhaps 150,000 were dead or missing, although there can be no certainty about the exact figures.[2]

Much depended on artillery. At Verdun the initial German bombardment had been heavier and more comprehensive than anything previously seen on either side, and it went far towards creating the early successes. In later days the French in turn would manage to concentrate far more heavy and medium guns than they had in 1915, with ever increasing supplies of ammunition, so they were at last able to fight back on terms much nearer equality. Especially in their great counter-offensives in the autumn and winter of 1916, they finally achieved a virtuosity in this field that represented a very significant advance over their earlier practice. The late October operation to recapture Douaumont was an object lesson in methodical offensive tactics, which clearly showed that the Germans no longer held the upper hand in that department. It also made the name of General Nivelle, who had been in tactical command at Verdun since 1 May and who now organized the spectacularly successful creeping barrages which carried forward the counter-offensive.

The politically plausible Nivelle was almost instantly hailed as the new man. On 27 December he replaced Joffre as French commander-in-chief, jumping over the head of the more experienced Pétain to plan the disastrously over-optimistic offensive for April 1917 which would forever carry his name. Essentially his attack would be on a greater scale than any seen since 1914; but despite all the experiences of 1915–16 it would reject the proven techniques of 'bite and hold' tactics, and revert to the now discredited hope of a quick break-through. Meanwhile on the German side von Falkenhayn had only too obviously run out of ideas, and had been dismissed on 28 August. The command team of Field Marshal Paul von Hindenburg and General Erich von Ludendorff were brought in from the Eastern Front to replace him, and they would remain in post for the remainder of the war. Ludendorff, in particular, would make himself the most powerful man in Germany, so no small part of his country's final defeat must be laid at his door.

If the battle of Verdun marked the 'changing of the guard' in the high commands of the two sides, it was also a watershed between the tactical fumbling of the first half of the war, and the more focused and effective tactics of the second half. Before it, the generals had been feeling their way in a very novel military landscape, and usually with very inadequate material means. If they could then be condemned as 'butchers and bunglers', they did at least have the excuse that they lacked the necessary resources, and in any case no one else knew any better. There was, of course, plenty of necessary bluster to the effect that everyone in authority knew exactly what they were doing; but in reality they did not and could not possibly have done. After Verdun and the Somme, by contrast, the shape of modern tactics had become considerably less mysterious. New techniques had been tried and proved, such as intense rehearsals before any attack, the widespread use of gas shell, and the creeping barrage. A new generation of middle-ranking officers was also being promoted who had seen modern warfare at close hand, bringing fresh ideas about how it should be tackled. There were therefore fewer excuses than there had been for ignorance or bad practice. The higher commanders now had a pretty good idea of what they were supposed to do, even if they were not always able to carry it off successfully.

Outside the narrow confines of the Verdun battlefield, the various campaigns against Turkey were all in the doldrums, and there was stalemate and trenchlock on the Italian front, where numerous offensives against the Austrians were blocked on the river Isonzo. In the North Sea the long-expected great naval battle between the British and German fleets was finally fought at Jutland from 31 May to 1 June 1916. It ended in a draw, which was deeply frustrating to a British public that was avid for a new Trafalgar; but it was actually still more frustrating to the *Kriegsmarine*, whose surface fleet could not, after all, break out of the allied blockade. It found itself confined to its bases for the remainder of the war, thereby inexorably increasing both the disaffection of its sailors and the strategic demand for unrestricted submarine warfare.

CHAPTER FOUR

The Battle of the Somme, 1916

The Battle of the Somme, 1916

Before the Germans attacked Verdun in February, the big allied push in the West for 1916 had been planned for the area of the Somme, on a fresh battlefield at the junction between the main French and British contingents. In the original plan the French were to have had almost twice as many troops in line as the untested British New Armies; but in the event the insatiable demands of Verdun meant they would have only about half as many. The battle of Verdun seriously reduced the French contingent that could fight on the Somme, and so it placed a proportionally heavier responsibility on the British. Equally, Haig was placed under repeated French pressure to bring forward the starting date of his attack. He had originally intended to begin the battle in mid-August, but was eventually persuaded to go in late June, with the week-long preliminary bombardment actually starting on the 24th. Technically speaking, this was the real 'first day of the Somme', although in popular usage that title has always been given to 1 July, the day when the infantry finally went over the top. At least the infrastructure of the offensive had been intensively prepared over the course of several months, with a much bigger build-up of troops and supplies than the BEF had previously dreamed of. By this time allied air superiority was massive, as was the sheer weight of artillery ammunition ready to be fired. Unfortunately, however, the scale of these enormous preparations completely ruled out any possibility of surprise. The Germans knew exactly where the big push would be launched, and they were more than ready to receive it.

For the British army, 1 July turned out to be the very worst day in its whole history, since it suffered some 58,000 casualties of which about 19,000 were dead.[1] The figure 58,000 represented almost a fifth of the total strength of the pre-war regular army (and incidentally no less than half of the army in 2007), although it should also be said that on 1 July 1916 it represented only something between 1 and 2 per cent of the mobilized total of British Empire forces worldwide. But whatever statistics one compares it with, the total was nevertheless horrific, and arguably doubly so when contrasted with the French loss of just 8,000 total casualties on the same day for a considerably greater gain in captured ground. Their Sixth Army reached the gates of Péronne within the next two weeks, and by October their methodical 'bite and hold' attacks were still allowing them to capture more real estate than their more numerous British allies. The experience of Verdun had clearly taught the French some vital tactical tricks that the British had not yet come to understand, so they might have been forgiven for repeating their commentary on their allies of the Light Brigade at Balaklava in the Crimean War – 'It is magnificent: but it is not war.'

The problem was not so much that the British had failed to keep abreast of the latest tactical theories but that, for want of practical experience, they had failed to translate them into effective action at the lowest levels. All but two of the British infantry divisions that attacked on 1 July were part of General Henry Rawlinson's Fourth Army, which had received a comprehensive and sensible tactical briefing manual in May, known as 'the Red Book'. However, the Red Book crucially failed to establish the detailed arrangements needed to co-ordinate artillery with infantry, and in particular exactly how much 'destruction' could realistically be expected from the preliminary bombardment.

On 1 July the general assumption was that the British artillery would have physically destroyed the Germans' front line by the bombardment, after which the infantry would simply walk across no man's land to occupy their wrecked trenches. There were, however, a number of problems with this expectation. The first was that in the hangover from the shell shortage of 1915 there was still too little HE shell, although there was now plenty of shrapnel. Shrapnel was designed to explode in the air and scatter the ground with steel balls each about half an inch in diameter. This was ideal for hitting men in the open, but it was not good for cutting wire entanglements and hopeless for destroying fortifications. HE was much better against fortifications, if it was available, but still not very good against wire. In 1916 the British fuses detonated only after the shell had buried itself in the ground, which limited the horizontal blast needed to disrupt entanglements. It would be only halfway through 1917 that a new fuse (Type 106) was produced which detonated immediately

The Battle of the Somme, 1916

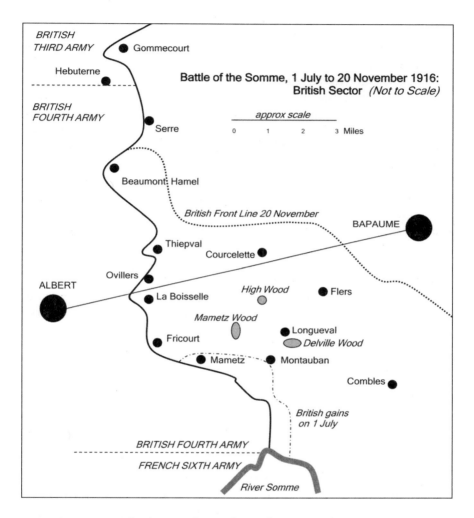

BRITISH
THIRD ARMY
Gommecourt

Hebuterne

BRITISH
FOURTH ARMY

Serre

Beaumont Hamel

British Front Line 20 November

BAPAUME

Thiepval
Courcelette

Ovillers

ALBERT

La Boisselle

High Wood

Flers

Mametz Wood

Fricourt

Longueval
Delville Wood

Mametz

Montauban

Combles

British gains
on 1 July

BRITISH FOURTH ARMY

FRENCH SIXTH ARMY

River Somme

Battle of the Somme, 1 July to 20 November 1916: British Sector *(Not to Scale)*

approx scale

0   1   2   3 Miles

upon impact with the earth, making for a much superior weapon against wire. On 1 July on the Somme, however, a significant proportion of the German wire that should have been cut by the artillery was not cut.

The lack of sufficient HE shell on the Somme also meant that even after a week's bombardment the front two lines of German trenches were far from totally destroyed. The ratio of British guns per mile of front remained less than it had been at Neuve Chapelle fifteen months earlier, especially since there were now two lines of enemy fortifications to be destroyed, rather than just one, and the attack frontage was now some eighteen miles, rather than just two. Thus the expectation that the attacker's artillery could physically annihilate the defending enemy turned out to be sadly misplaced. It was an expectation upon which the whole plan had rested, and so the first lesson of 1 July was that fire for 'destructive' effect could not work unless a very great deal more artillery could be provided than was actually the case. What was really needed, although it was not fully understood on this day, was fire for 'neutralizing' effect, or in other words some form of creeping barrage.

The creeping barrage was a system by which a line of shells was fired to explode about 50 yards in front of attacking infantry as they advanced, so that any defending enemy ahead of them would be 'neutralized' – that is, they would want to keep their heads down and thus be unable to fire their weapons before the moment when they were overrun by troops with rifles, bombs and bayonets. Every few minutes the line of shells would be aimed a little further forward, typically advancing by 100 yards every four minutes, although the exact rate could be altered to suit local conditions. On the first day of the Somme this technique was still very much in its infancy, and its potential was not yet properly understood, although that would change dramatically on the 'second day' (or at least by 14 July) and thereafter. By 1917 the whole art and science of the creeping barrage would be developed to a massive degree, with some examples having not just one or two lines of advancing shells, but as many as eight, reaching as far as 2,000 yards ahead of the attacking infantry, to ensure the maximum suppression of the defence. The mixture would also often be thickened up with mortars and massed machine gun fire, and increasingly with HE and then smoke shells, rather than merely shrapnel, as stocks gradually became available. Thus a 'creeping barrage' in mid-1917 would become a far more potent weapon of neutralization than anything seen a year earlier.

The Battle of the Somme, 1916

On 1 July 1916 the three divisions of XIII Corps on the extreme right wing of the British attack – and nearest to the battle-experienced French – did use creeping barrages. They made reasonable headway as a result, albeit still falling far short of the wilder expectations of the high command. But the remaining divisions further to the north did not use creepers, and so they were mostly shot down before they had advanced very far from their starting trenches. Whenever there was empty time between the ending of the preliminary bombardment (including the detonation of mines) and the start of the infantry attack, the defending German machine gunners would almost always be able to emerge from their bunkers, man their guns and open a blistering fire against anyone they found in front of them. This usually created mass slaughter, especially where the lack of a creeping barrage coincided with uncut German wire and naive or at least inexperienced attacking troops.

The tragedy seemed to be multiplied by the uniquely local nature of some of the volunteer battalions that made up Kitchener's New Armies. When the Accrington Pals were mown down at Serre, or the 36th Ulster Division at the Schwaben redoubt, it was not just a military unit that was destroyed, but the manhood of a whole tight-knit urban community. These troops were 'pals' in more than name, since they had all volunteered at the same time and the same place, and sometimes all from the same trades. Their murderous introduction to modern battle set up many local reverberations that can still be felt even today.

No one could hide the fact that 1 July was a disaster of epic proportions for the British, and in subsequent years it has gone far to confirm the widespread belief that all the generals of the Great War were butchers and bunglers. This impression would soon be reinforced when Haig attempted to follow through the infantry attack with a pre-programmed 'cavalry breakthrough' which, in the event, achieved nothing of the sort. From today's perspective it is easy to mock the whole idea of using cavalry on any modern battlefield, just as it is easy to sneer at some of the generals as hopelessly 'horsey' characters who derived their ideas from the nineteenth century, if not the eighteenth. This would be unfair: Haig, for example, was a leading advocate of all types of new technology, ranging from the motor car before the war to the Royal Flying Corps in 1915 and the tank in 1916. Nor was it necessarily stupid to think in terms of cavalry for exploiting a breakthrough. It could, after all, move considerably faster than men on foot, and it could keep on moving for far longer than any of the tanks that would be developed during the war. It would remain at the heart of any planning for a 'Corps de Chasse' to break through to the green fields on the far side of the slugging infantry battle. This was certainly the case in the early stages of the Somme battle, and would be again at Arras and Cambrai in 1917. Indeed, it almost worked on all three occasions. For example, some of the infantry who witnessed the attempted cavalry breakthrough towards High Wood on 14 July were convinced that there had been a genuine gap in the enemy lines that could have been exploited. However, as so often in this war, the tactical signalling from front to rear of the battlefield was defective which meant that too little cavalry arrived too late, and with inadequate higher command and control.

THE LONG HAUL

Despite the failure of the Corps de Chasse on 14 July, it was on that day that the British began to get their act together and make some genuine progress. A night attack with full use of creeping barrages ensured the capture of Bazentin and Longueval, although this in turn triggered a ferocious series of German counter-attacks. The fighting then continued at exceptionally high intensity, with much butchery and bungling on both sides. In particular the British high command often insisted on making attacks on too short a frontage and with inadequate time for planning, let alone rehearsals. On both counts this was running against good tactical practice, and it created repeated defeats as well as thousands of unnecessary casualties. On the German side there was no less profligacy with men's lives, as their system of automatic counter-attacks on every occasion locked them into ever mounting attrition. The British would gradually become

The Battle of the Somme, 1916

expert in predicting these counter-attacks very accurately, and in arranging crushing artillery bombardments against them.

Both literally and metaphorically the Somme battlefield may be seen as a hill up which the British had to climb. Many of the original front-line trenches were on relatively low-lying ground, overlooked and dominated by German positions further to the east, especially at High Wood and Delville Wood. Haig and Rawlinson had hoped to capture these gentle hills in the first two days of the battle, so that General Hubert Gough's mobile Corps de Chasse, which would later be designated the Fifth Army, could immediately break through to Bapaume and beyond. In the event, however, it took many weeks of the most gruelling fighting even to reach the crestline. The battle ebbed and flowed over those key features, with huge heartbreak and many tens of thousands of casualties along the way. It was only in the big push of 15 September (officially known as the battle of Flers-Courcelette) that the allies were finally able to start downhill on the far side, some two and a half months later than they had originally hoped.

Apart from anything else, the battle of Flers-Courcelette was memorable because it saw the first use of tanks in combat. During 1915 they had been very much in the prototype and development phase, and in the first half of 1916 they were still suffering 'teething troubles' and difficulties in production. Thus on 15 September only forty-nine could be put in the field, and of these only thirteen actually managed to get into action. It has to be said that they did not do particularly well. The tactics designed for them demanded gaps to be left in the creeping barrage, which immediately caused great problems for their supporting infantry. They did nevertheless succeed in capturing the village of Flers, which made an iconic moment for the press, although even then they overshot and found that the infantry could not keep up with them. Haig, and everyone else who was militarily involved, recognized that a great deal of further work needed to be done, not only mechanically on the tanks themselves, but also intellectually on their tactics. However, he had full confidence that all this would happen in the fullness of time, so he immediately placed an order for a further 1,000 of the futuristic machines.[2]

Nor were tanks the only improvement in tactics for the offensive, since by this time the British were well on the way to perfecting their creeping barrages, as well as many aspects of infantry fighting. For example, with their Lewis guns they had taken the lead in the deployment of light machine guns that could be carried relatively easily within every platoon. Their Stokes mortar was also the international leader in its class. Hard-won combat experience was slowly percolating through every level of command, with tangibly improved technique as the long-awaited result. Nevertheless, the second half of the Somme battle lasted until 18 November, and still there was no breakthrough. This is the part of the battle that has often been forgotten. It was a time when forward progress was generally little better than it had been before, and the Germans continued to build new rearward lines of trenches until, at the end of the battle, they had completed no fewer than seven. It was also a time when the weather deteriorated until the battlefield eventually became a quagmire in which any sort of movement was extremely difficult. The mud and high water table at Ypres in late 1917 has become notorious in the popular imagination, but it is less well known that something similar had already happened a year earlier on the Somme. The sunny and well-drained chalk battlefield of July had turned into a morass of glutinous goo by November. Eventually the battle had to be closed down simply because it was no longer possible to move forward the munitions needed to keep it going. There would thus be no breakthrough in 1916, although the prospect of one always continued to tantalize tacticians.

Meanwhile the 'grinding down' of the German army continued inexorably until it finally suffered almost two-thirds of a million casualties, or nearly twice as many as at Verdun.[3] This made a profound impression upon the German troops, who were forced to retreat from one trench line to another, week by week and month by month. They also saw allied aircraft flying freely overhead, photographing every position and calling down increasingly accurate artillery fire, whereas the Luftwaffe was rarely able to penetrate behind allied lines. The Germans gradually began to lose the assumption of ultimate victory that had so powerfully buoyed up their morale during the first half of the war.[4]

Particularly shocking was the sheer weight of impersonal shelling that was now being concentrated against them. In his memoirs, the remarkable infantry subaltern Ernst Jünger repeatedly emphasized 'the overwhelming effects of the war of material. We had to adapt ourselves to an entirely new phase of war.'[5] He went on, 'after the battle of the Somme the war had its own peculiar impress that distinguished it from all other wars. After this battle the German soldier wore the steel helmet, and in his features there were chiselled the lines of an energy stretched to the utmost pitch.'[6] 'Chivalry here took a final farewell. It had to yield to the heightened intensity of war, just as all fine and personal feeling has to yield when machinery gets the upper hand.'[7]

Admittedly, the allies lost about the same total of killed and wounded as their opponents. A third of them were French, making almost as great a loss as they had suffered at Verdun itself, which went far towards sapping their morale for 1917.[8] In the case of the British, the battle of the Somme represented their first truly serious 'butcher's bill' so far in the war. In one perspective this meant it could be psychologically supported more easily, because it had not been preceded by almost two years of intense attrition, as had been the case for the French. Yet on the other hand, the sheer shock, novelty and scale of the losses struck a major blow to confidence, both throughout the army and among the wider public.

In all armies the uncritical optimism of August 1914 was visibly melting away, as the full horror of *der Millionenkrieg* in the industrial age gradually sank into the minds of all participants. The personal letters and diaries of soldiers became ever more bitter and disillusioned, especially if the authors had witnessed the chaos of 1915, which had been considerably less focused or purposeful than the tactics seen at either Verdun or the Somme by the end of 1916. It is noticeable that, at least in the British case, a considerable majority of the poets and autobiographers whose work subsequently rose to prominence had already been in the trenches during 1915. It was that particular generation that had gone to war with the highest hopes, and which therefore sank to the lowest depths when the horrific realities became impossibly overwhelming.

The Roman poet Virgil (70–19 BC) began his great work *The Aeneid* with the immortal phrase 'Arms and the man I sing' (Arma virumque cano), and warfare has often been the theme of great literature ever since. Rarely, however, has a group of writers made a more powerful impact with their poems and memoirs on this subject than the British authors who served in the trenches during the Great War. Germany had her Erich Maria Remarque, whose *Im Westen nichts Neues (All Quiet on the Western Front)* was first published in 1929.[9] France had her Henri Barbusse with *Le Feu*.[10] The USA had such figures as John Dos Passos, who first came to prominence with *Three Soldiers* in 1921, and Ernest Hemingway with *A Farewell to Arms* in 1929. Yet it is surely the British writers who have dominated this particular genre from the late 1920s, when their work first began to be known, right through to the present day. The power of their writings lies in a compelling combination of intimate human observations, bitterness against the high command, and generosity in mourning – all often informed by the classical literature that was so central to the educational system of their age. As an example, Wilfred Owen's acid question, 'What passing bells for those who die as cattle? Only the monstrous anger of the guns',[11] evokes the quiet eighteenth-century English country churchyard of Gray's *Elegy*, at the same time as it reminds us of the mass slaughter and unacceptable, unavoidable, deadly impersonality of the Western Front. Owen was an officer who grieved for his men and was incandescently angry at the treatment they were receiving, but who also had the ability to place it all in the context of the English literary canon.[12]

The all-professional British army of the nineteenth century had been notably remote from civilian society, and especially from the middle classes. It had numbered only around a third of a million men, whereas in the Great War this state of affairs changed dramatically and radically. Over six million men suddenly came under arms, which meant that many sections of society that had never previously been exposed to military life found themselves living in trenches 'up to their eyes in muck and bullets'. This was a traumatic experience

The Battle of the Somme, 1916

that came as a great shock not only to the individuals concerned, but especially to the civilians at home who had never previously had the horrors of military life explained to them by 'their own kind'. A central element in the exquisite poignancy of British war poetry was that it was written by gentle men from educated backgrounds. Whether they were officers or other ranks, middle-class or working-class, the whole business of soldiering and warfare was essentially repugnant to them. Almost all of them had volunteered to fight, and some of them, such as Siegfried Sassoon, even made very good soldiers. However, none of that made them love the war that they actually found on the Western Front. It turned out to be so very different from what anyone had expected that they reacted to it with anger, incomprehension and, often, deep depression.

In 1914 it had been some of the highest commanders who had suffered the most significant nervous breakdowns, but by late 1916 the phenomenon had become widespread among officers and men at every level. 'Shell shock', which had been predicted theoretically ever since the original invention of High Explosives, now became an everyday occurrence. Far too often its existence was denied and even mistaken for 'cowardice', which could lead to fatal results for sufferers, who found themselves facing a court martial.[13] We must remember that the whole science of psychiatry was still very much in its infancy. The modern understanding of Post-Traumatic Stress Disorder (PTSD) was still a long way in the future. Nevertheless, the novel and unrelenting horrors of the great trench war, and their effect on the minds of soldiers, were starting to be seen as a factor of military importance in a way that had never previously been the case.

CHAPTER FIVE

Spring 1917

Spring 1917

THE HINDENBURG LINE

At the end of the battles of Verdun and the Somme, the armies on the Western Front took stock, braced themselves for another winter in the freezing mud of the trenches, and laid their plans for spring 1917. The first of these emerged at a conference in Calais on 26–27 February in which the new British prime minister, David Lloyd George, enthusiastically endorsed the heady optimism of his new-found friend Nivelle, in an attempt to bypass the British generals and reduce their political power. This initiative immediately created bad feeling between himself and his army that would persist throughout the remainder of the war, and indeed beyond. Still more seriously, news arrived that the Tsar had been forced to abdicate on 15 March. At first this did not appear to affect the Russians' war effort, since General Brusilov mounted his second major offensive on 1 July, but after that failed it soon became clear that desertion and mutiny were taking over the Russian armies. However, the USA entered the war against Germany on 6 April, following Ludendorff's declaration of unrestricted submarine warfare. This promised to give a great boost to the allies in France in 1918, although logistics experts were pain-fully aware of just how long it would take the Americans to mobilize their full fighting strength. It would be more realistic to expect them to exert decisive leverage only in 1919, rather than 1918.

On the Western Front itself the first major event was a carefully organized German retreat to 'shorten their line' and to occupy pre-viously prepared positions behind the Noyon salient. These new fortifications were known as 'the Hindenburg Line', and they were formidable, incorporating all the lessons that the Germans had learned from their sacrificial defensive battles in the previous autumn. Ever greater depth between trench lines was a central feature of the system, together with numerous small strongpoints ahead of them, between them and behind them. The plan was no longer to beat the enemy off from a fragile front line, but rather to suck him into the middle of an interlocking 'web' of defences. Ideally these would be sited on reverse slopes, where the attackers' artillery observers could no longer follow the course of the battle, but where the overwatching defender's artillery could make free play. Then, once the attack had become confused and fragmented, there would be counter-attacks at every level, designed to retake all the lost ground and send the attackers back to their start line with heavy loss. Two other important features of the new system were exceptionally thick belts of barbed wire, perhaps thirty feet deep, and a widespread programme of pouring reinforced concrete. The Germans began to build shell-proof shelters and machine gun nests at or close below ground level, to complement their existing deep bunkers. It would be a whole year before the allies began to copy this technique on any large scale.

The advantage of the Germans' big step back in February and March 1917 was partly that they could economize on manpower by

The German concept of 'defence in depth'. The outpost zone is designed to absorb the enemy's main artillery bombardment and to confuse his attacking infantry. The main battle zone will thus be preserved in a good state to defend itself against any new enemy impetus, but even if some parts of it are captured, counter-attacks at every level (shown here by arrows) will be launched immediately to recapture lost ground.

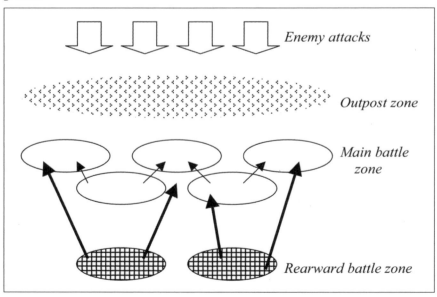

Enemy attacks

Outpost zone

Main battle zone

Rearward battle zone

shortening their line, but also that they were winning leisure to build their new fortifications properly and deliberately some way behind the front. The retreat was designed to cover the completion of the defensive work, so that it did not have to be improvised under enemy fire. The labourers could enjoy the luxury of working in daylight and free from interference. So effective were all these 'custom-built' fortifications that they would not be broken until late September 1918, apart from a brief escapade at Cambrai from 20 to 30 November 1917. Even in sectors where the Germans did not step back, for example around Ypres, the very concept of their 'depth defence' still meant that they could construct many of their pillboxes and bunkers on reverse slopes some way behind the front, and thus still relatively well protected from enemy interference during the building phase. The main designer of these fortifications was General Friedrich Sixt von Arnim, who had studied defensive warfare at close hand on the Somme in 1916 and who then took command of the Fourth Army around Ypres in 1917. It would not be too much to suggest that he, more than any other individual apart perhaps from Lloyd George in 1918, placed the most obstacles in the path of Haig's success in command of the BEF on the Western Front.

The great step back to the Hindenburg Line was nevertheless still a retreat rather than a step forward. The Germans who were ordered to abandon all the trenches they had painfully built and defended during the last days of the Somme battle were not persuaded that this was a sign of impending victory. They did their best to draw satisfaction from the operation by leaving booby traps and insulting graffiti behind them as they left, for the allies who followed them up to discover, but they could not help reflecting that the retreat began only three months after the Somme had finished. This powerfully suggested that the Somme had really been a defeat, and the Germans had hung around the battlefield for a while merely to satisfy their honour, in rather the same way that General Robert E Lee had kept his army on the field of Gettysburg for a day after that battle ended. By contrast, the allies who followed up the German retreat in spring 1917 did not experience any sense of victory after such a gruelling and bloody engagement, and were further shocked to encounter the novel

The Great War on the Western Front

'frightfulness' of booby traps used on an unprecedented scale. In most British accounts these weapons are seen as just one more murderous type of attrition, and no connection is made with the idea that the BEF might have won on the Somme. But then again, neither had the Army of the Potomac at first realized that it had won at Gettysburg in 1863.

Meanwhile the allies had planned a big new co-ordinated offensive for spring 1917, which had to be delayed because of the German retreat. Eventually it started with a British diversionary push at Arras and Vimy Ridge on 9 April. Then on 16 April the French were to make a devastating attack (which would become known as the 'Nivelle Offensive') on the Chemin des Dames – the long ridge running just north of the river Aisne that the Germans had turned into a fortress immediately after their retreat from the Marne in 1914.

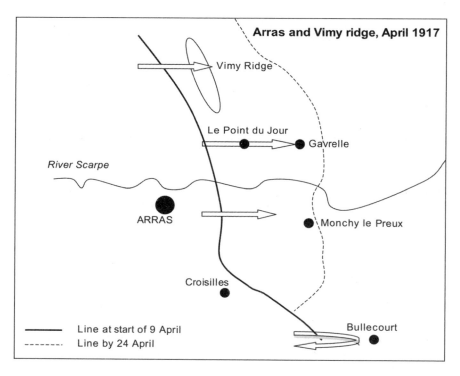

Spring 1917

At Arras the 'first day' of the attack went off far more successfully than the 'first day of the Somme' on 1 July 1916. Despite the loss of air superiority, it was informed by nine months of intense combat experience, such as had not at first been available to the British on the Somme. Therefore the new artillery preparation was much more carefully orchestrated, with much more HE and even smoke shells in some of the creeping barrages. The preliminary bombardment with almost 3,000 guns lasted three weeks, and one observer called it 'the greatest barrage ever seen'. Also the infantry spearheads were much better trained to take advantage of it, and in several places they were able to march forward some 6,000 yards without suffering heavy casualties. When they first heard of this unprecedented advance, the German high command was rocked to the core.

The capture of Vimy Ridge by the Canadian corps, commanded by General Julian Byng, was a meticulously prepared feat of arms that has been particularly celebrated by the Canadian government. The battlefield park that has been created there is always worth a visit nowadays. The original craters from mines and shells have not been ploughed over, as they have been on most of the other battlefields, so the tourist can gain a vivid impression of just how deep they are and how they must have looked before the vegetation grew back. More to the point is their sheer numbers packed into a relatively small area, often with two or more craters overlapping each other. This contrasts with the Newfoundland battlefield park on the Somme battlefield, where the shell holes are noticeably smaller and much further apart – although of course the shrapnel that was so widely used there did not leave craters. At Vimy there is no avoiding the physical evidence that a much heavier weight of HE shell was fired, and in fact during the first week of the Arras battle as a whole the British fired a total of slightly more than two million shells.

This awesome firepower helped forward more than just the Canadians, since the 'home-grown' British divisions on their right flank also did very well. In particular the 9th Scottish Division's capture of Le Point du Jour (north of Athies) was a remarkable achievement, combining careful planning and deception with numbing firepower on the day. This allowed the infantry to walk over the enemy's defences with slight loss, at least until the dread moment arrived when the attackers had outrun the reach of their guns and had come up against the enemy's second line. South of that there was a similar story, assisted by the medieval tunnels under the city of Arras, which had been improved to give shelter and concealment to the assault troops as they moved forward almost to the front line. They were also helped by the fact that the Germans, smarting from the devastating defeat of so many of their counter-attacks on the Somme, had left their counter-attack forces at Arras too far to the rear to be able to intervene. Thus the British were able to make dramatic advances before they encountered serious resistance. Nevertheless, in every case the Germans consolidated along their second line, and the fighting degenerated into the familiar see-saw with escalating casualties on both sides.

After the 'first day' at Arras there would be no more dramatic advances. The cavalry failed to break through at Monchy le Preux, and the infantry spearheads bogged down, waiting for their essential artillery support to catch up. It also soon became clear that in this 'Bloody April' the balance of power in the air was starting to swing back to the Germans, as their aircraft took a technological lead, most notably with their Albatross series of multi-role combat planes. This trend would grow through the summer as new specialized types were deployed such as the Halberstadt fighter bomber for ground attack, and of course the famous Fokker DR1 triplane air superiority fighter, which would be immortalized by the 'Red Baron' Manfred von Richthofen.

If the allies were perfecting their art of attack on the ground, they had not yet won the wider technological war. When we look to the south of the city of Arras in April 1917, for example, we do not find a favourable situation for the British. In this area the northernmost sector of the Hindenburg Line had been built and occupied earlier in the year, which made for more formidable German defences than at Vimy Ridge and Le Point du Jour. The British experienced a further difficulty because this was also the site of the boundary between General Edmund Allenby's Third Army, responsible for the bulk of the battle, and Gough's Fifth Army on the right flank. Gough would attack later than Allenby, mainly around Bullecourt on 9–11 April, where he had some innovative ideas about tactics. In a concept somewhat similar to Sir John French's trust in gas at Loos in 1915, he wanted to base a major part of his plan upon an all but untried new technology – in this case the tank. Unfortunately, however, his intended surprise required the Australian assault infantry to lie out in no man's land overnight, so that they would be present and ready to accompany the tanks when they crushed the enemy defences at dawn. These arrangements might have worked well if only there had not been freezing snow on the ground, and if only the tanks – which had been briefed and ordered forward very late in the day, and in a blizzard – had managed to arrive on time. Neither of these conditions was met, so that very soon after dawn a very cold and disaffected group of Australians expressed their contempt for all tanks in general, and for incompetent Pommy staffwork in particular. Their reward was to be told that they would have to go through the whole exercise all over again on the second night, which stoked them up from 'furious' to 'incandescent'. Then, when the attack finally did go in, it enjoyed only very limited success and suffered heavy casualties, which only confirmed the ANZACs in their forcibly expressed opinions.

THE NIVELLE OFFENSIVE

All the fighting at Vimy, Arras and Bullecourt had, of course, been designed as merely a diversion and an overture to help the great French 'Nivelle Offensive' on the Chemin des Dames, and it is true that it did indeed shock the enemy commanders by its initial depth of penetration. What it could not and did not do, however, was to fool them about Nivelle's intention to make a massive attack on the Aisne. He was assembling no fewer than 50 divisions and 5,000 guns on that sector, which were totally impossible to conceal. There was no possibility of surprise, any more than there had been in most of the previous battles in this war. It would be only at Cambrai on 20 November 1917 that the techniques of 'predicted artillery fire' would allow an attack to be mounted without a long preliminary period of shelling in the days before the infantry actually went over the top. Such prolonged bombardments (one week on the Somme, three weeks at Arras, two weeks at Third Ypres) represented unmissable clues to the enemy that something big was afoot. He would thus be able to amass his reserves in good time, and adjust his plans accordingly.

The French plans for their assault were further compromised when the Germans captured a copy of them on 5 April, at a time when all of Nivelle's immediate military subordinates, as well as his political superiors, were in any case experiencing grave doubts about the whole project. Even he himself momentarily offered to resign. Vital low-level details in planning the attack were being sacrificed in the interests of its vastly excessive scale and optimism. Yet as far as the soldiers at lower levels were concerned, all they got was repeated reassurance from Nivelle himself that this 'one last push' would finish the war completely, and all within the space of a few days. They accepted this official rationale with both relief and hope, and indeed who can possibly blame them?

The trouble was that the Germans had prepared their Chemin des Dames battlefield in much better depth than they had managed to do at Vimy Ridge and Arras. Nor did it help that the weather was freezing and many of the combats were fought in driving sleet. The attacking French troops were sucked into a morass of defensive strongpoints in which they lost the support of their own artillery at the same time as they came under fire from all directions, and were finally counter-attacked with devastating effect. They did gain large tracts of ground, although it was mostly ground that the enemy was happy to sacrifice, but the French also suffered very heavy losses indeed. By this point in the war they had suffered a grand total of well over three million casualties, and were morally as well as physically exhausted. Nivelle was replaced as commander-in-chief by Pétain on 15 May, with General Ferdinand Foch as his Chief of Staff. More to the point, however, was the widespread shock of realization that Nivelle's confident promises of a rapid decision had never been more than hot air and wind. Disillusionment and a sense of betrayal sud-

Spring 1917

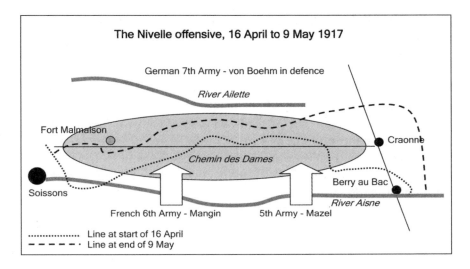

The Nivelle offensive, 16 April to 9 May 1917

German 7th Army - von Boehm in defence

River Ailette

Fort Malmaison

Chemin des Dames

Craonne

Soissons

Berry au Bac

River Aisne

French 6th Army - Mangin   5th Army - Mazel

.... Line at start of 16 April
— — — — · Line at end of 9 May

denly spread throughout the French army, and widespread mutinies were not slow to follow.

The amazing thing about the French mutinies and combat refusals was that they were successfully hidden from the Germans, and secrecy was maintained. This was partly because many of the protesting troops agreed to hold the line defensively, but refused to make any attack. Therefore from the Germans' point of view the French lines remained fully garrisoned. In any case they had to worry about the next Russian offensive, as well as a major British push that was developing in the Ypres sector. It was also of crucial importance that Pétain understood the soul of the French soldier, and knew how to act quickly to stop the rot. By making a few stern examples of the most intransigent mutineers he was merely following conventional military culture, but in other areas he was imaginative, innovative and humane. He improved the provision of food (and wine, or *pinard*); he increased home leave and arranged a regular rotation of rests out of the line; and he did what he could to increase the soldiers' battered self-esteem. Above all, he banned sacrificial attacks in which lives would be wantonly thrown away to no obvious purpose. The French army would revert largely to the defensive for the next twelve

months, although it continued to practise limited and carefully prepared 'bite and hold' operations in circumstances where it was
confident the casualties would be light. One such attack was the final
recapture of the 'Le Mort Homme' feature and other advanced positions at Verdun on 20 August; another was a very tightly controlled
and successful operation at Malmaison on 23–26 October. However,
the French would venture forth to make larger attacks only in 1918,
and only when they enjoyed clear tactical advantages. They had
already lost many more men than either the British or the Germans in
the West, and they quite reasonably believed it was high time for
others to take up the lethal burden.

One source of reinforcements was 'la force noire', that is, the
troops raised in the French colonies in North Africa, sub-Saharan
Africa and sometimes even further afield. Alas, by mid-1917 most
of the best of these had already been consumed in the flames of combat, with widely varying degrees of tactical success. They had nevertheless left an indelible mark upon the character of the French army
as a whole, not least through the personalities of some of their leading commanders who rose to high office in the Great War. Joffre
himself was the outstanding example, but the doyen of colonial
officers was Joseph Galliéni, who played a key role defending Paris in
1914. Charles 'Butcher' Mangin grew into one of the most effective
fighting generals at Verdun and then in 1918, although he was a
spiritual ally of Nivelle, as perhaps his nickname might suggest. Less
successful was the legendary Hubert Lyautey, the French equivalent
to Kitchener, who was brought in from his private fiefdom in
Morocco in late 1916 to become Minister of War, only to be instru-
mental in bringing down the whole government in March 1917. This
did not prevent his promotion to Marshal in 1921 and his eventual
elevation to the highest honour any French, or indeed Corsican,
officer can legally claim – namely a prestigious tomb in Les Invalides
in Paris.

Other reinforcements came from some unexpected sources. A
brigade of Russians fought in the Champagne, east of Reims, where
their chapel may still be visited. Portugal entered the fighting on
9 March 1916, but she could deploy only two divisions, or approxi-

mately the same numbers as the Indian Army forces (the British equivalent to 'la force noire'), who had fought well in 1914–15, but had then melted away. In the summer of 1917 the Americans were still far from arriving in significant strength. All this meant that there was really only one force that could take the pressure off the French in the moment of their post-Nivelle crisis, and that was the BEF of the British Empire.

By this time the BEF had entered its phase of maximum strength and was also, at long last, well on the way to perfecting its art of modern war. It had already demonstrated this on the 'first day' of Arras and was about to do so again, perhaps more effectively still, on 7 June: the 'first day' of Messines.

CHAPTER SIX

Passchendaele

Passchendaele

The attack on the Wytschaete-Messines ridge was a limited 'bite and hold' operation designed to clear the southern flank of the forthcoming Third Battle of Ypres. Messines was meticulously planned by General Herbert Plumer, who had taken to heart the key lesson of the Somme, that careful rehearsal and comprehensive planning were even more important than massive artillery bombardments. Plumer kept a firm personal grip on every possible aspect of his operation, from the barrage plan to the co-ordination of the mines, and from the water supply to the new backpacks used to take supplies to the front. The Australian general John Monash once famously said that trench warfare was 'simply a problem of engineering', and the battle of Messines, at which he was present as a division commander, was doubtless the sort of thing that he had in mind.

Plumer certainly believed in overkill, with some three million shells being fired during the two-week preliminary bombardment that was designed not only to break the Germans' wire, but even to starve out their front-line infantry by preventing supplies being moved up to them from the rear. Then these supposedly starved troops would be blown sky-high by the simultaneous detonation of massive interlocking mines. The effects of the shock waves were to be multiplied as they rebounded off each other, and in the event as many as some 10,000 Germans were killed. The explosion could be heard in London, 130 miles away. Then a comprehensive creeping barrage began immediately and the attacking infantry captured the crest of the ridge along the whole of the attack frontage, at small loss. Casualties slowly mounted as the Germans gathered their wits and launched counter-attacks during the following days, complete with ground attack aircraft, but overall the battle had been a remarkable demonstration of Plumer's tactical virtuosity.

Unfortunately the same could not be said of the early stages of the next battle, which was to be a much larger offensive out of the Ypres salient and Nieuport. One of the problems was that the operation had multiple aims, the incongruous first of which was to help the Royal Navy by capturing enemy naval bases on the Belgian coast. A major bridgehead across the mouth of the Yser Canal was to be set up opposite Nieuport, from which a drive on Ostend and Zeebrugge could be launched in conjunction with amphibious landings. However, while the bridgehead was still garrisoned by only one brigade, the Germans very cleverly counter-attacked and wiped it out. It soon became clear that the whole coastal wing of the British offensive would have to be abandoned. If Ostend were to be captured at all, it would have to be taken by an overland thrust of almost thirty miles due north from the Ypres salient, rather than the ten miles north-east from Nieuport. This was, of course, very much further than had been achieved by any offensive on the Western Front since 1914. Even if the rail junction north of Roulers (Roeselare) were accepted as a compromise or intermediate target, it was still twelve miles north-east from Ypres, and in a divergent direction.

As if this confusion were not bad enough, a number of other conflicting aims were also jostling for attention. One was the tactical consideration that the best way to clear the Germans away from the Ypres area was to capture the Gheluvelt plateau to the east of the city, in the direction of Menin, which was commanding high ground. Thus Haig found he had three possible directions for his thrust – towards Ostend, Roulers or Menin – which was of course no more than the logical result of starting in a salient where the enemy occupied almost three out of the four points of the compass.

It was certainly Haig's duty to select one out of the three possible directions for his attack, and explain clearly to his subordinates exactly what the aim was intended to be. Alas, he failed to do either, but retreated into veiled talk of secret 'higher considerations' which prevented him from explaining his master plan. This has often been taken as a reference to the need to draw German attention away from the French mutinies, at a time when he felt he could not state out loud that they actually existed, in the same way that the Somme had relieved the pressure on Verdun in 1916. Modern research apparently rejects this interpretation of both 1916 and 1917, although of course Haig always saw it as his duty to fight alongside his French allies. Linked to all this, in Haig's mind there must also have been some sort of theory of attrition, or 'putting pressure on the Germans', which in

Passchendaele

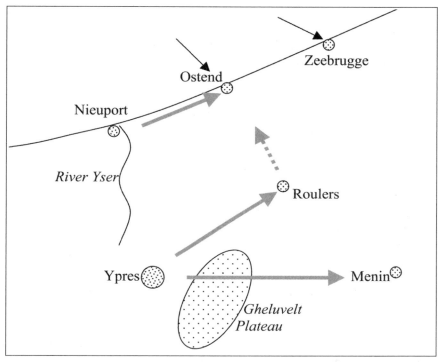

Haig's strategic objectives for Third Ypres. To capture Ostend his best option was to drive up the coast from Nieuport, supported by amphibious landings, but when that became impossible he would have to go from Ypres via Roulers. But to get out of Ypres at all it was best to start by clearing the Gheluvelt Plateau in the direction of Menin.

turn implied 'seeking to fight frontal battles with as many of them as possible', thereby 'killing as many of them as possible'. This, of course, was a totally different objective from the idea of making a clean and deep breakthrough to Ostend, or Roulers, or across the Gheluvelt plateau. In all his battles Haig invariably retained some ultimate faith in at least the possibility of such a breakthrough, although he never actually managed to achieve one. In the particular case of Third Ypres it meant that he appointed the cavalryman Gough to command the major part of the battle, while Plumer, the

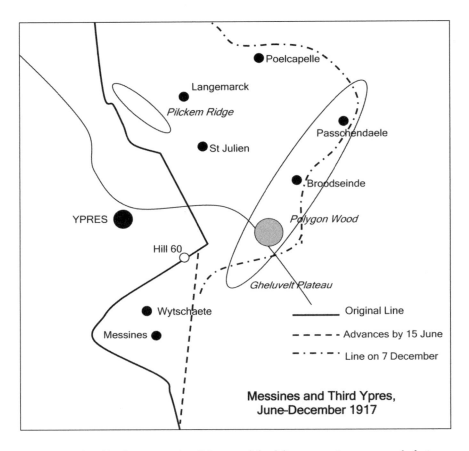

Messines and Third Ypres,
June–December 1917

more methodical expert in 'bite and hold' operations, was left in a secondary role.

There were thus considerable uncertainties within Haig's planning staff. In which direction should they attack, and should they go for a breakthrough or a limited objective? In the event an ingenious compromise was agreed, whereby a whole series of 'bite and hold' attacks would be mounted in quick succession, hopefully at three-day intervals, until perhaps a final decisive breakthrough might be achieved. As for the direction, it was optimistically believed that because the attack frontage would be so long, and the attacking troops so

Passchendaele

numerous, all the various different objectives could be captured, and so every point of the compass could be covered. It might even be said, with the benefit of hindsight, that if only the battle had started a month earlier, and if only the weather gods had bestowed a little bit more luck upon it, it just might have worked.

Behind all this, however, is the much darker question of why Haig should have chosen to fight at Ypres at all. Even if we accept that he absolutely had to fight a major battle somewhere – to relieve the French or even to make a breakthrough all the way to Berlin – we are still free to question his precise choice of battlefield. His battles around Arras had only just finished in May, so we can understand why he might not have wished to return to the charge in that particular area. Nor had he personally any good memories of the sector facing Lille, between Vimy and Armentières. Conversely, however, he must surely have treasured warm memories of his own personal triumph at the first (defensive) battle of Ypres in 1914. For Douglas Haig himself, the Ypres salient must have seemed almost like a benign environment, even though it was a notoriously malevolent one for those who had to actually live in it. Not only was it surrounded and overlooked on three sides by the enemy, and especially by his artillery, but it was a notoriously damp and muddy site in its own right. It had already won a particularly evil reputation among the rank and file of the BEF during Haig's first battle in 1914, which was not at all improved by the frightening German use of gas in the second battle in 1915.

There was, however, another potential site for the great midsummer offensive of 1917, which with today's hindsight we can suggest would have been considerably better than Ypres. This was the Cambrai sector, to the south of Arras, where the British were not in a salient and where the well-drained ground had not been churned up by years of shell fire. Admittedly it was a sector in which the Germans were especially well fortified in their new Hindenburg Line, but they were extremely well fortified at Ypres too, so maybe there was no significant disadvantage in that respect. As it happens, Cambrai would be the scene of a dramatic British success on 20 November, but by that time too many of the available resources had already been consumed in the Ypres salient. The Cambrai battle – really it should

77

be called little more than a 'raid' – could not be sustained for more than ten days. We may speculate that if only the main weight of the BEF had been deployed to Cambrai in midsummer, the overall level of success might have been very much higher than it actually was.

The reality, however, was that Haig had committed himself unshakeably to Ypres as the site of his main battle of 1917. Ideally it should have started very soon after the preliminaries at Messines in early June, but in fact it was delayed, for a variety of reasons, for over a month. The bombardment did not start until 18 July, at which point the Germans sprang their first nasty surprise, in the form of a counter-battery bombardment using their new blistering agent, mustard gas. The British artillery had to struggle against this horror at the same time as it was trying to suppress the German artillery, so naturally its efficiency was reduced. Finally the infantry went over the top on 31 July.

The first 'bite and hold' operation went very well over ground that had been thoroughly prepared by the artillery. However, it was found that the Germans had very strong positions in great depth, including many concrete bunkers, and it was only their forward outposts that had been captured. Then it began to rain, and the rain did not stop before the battlefield had been turned into a total quagmire. The preparations for the second 'bite' were delayed, and it turned out to be far less decisive than the first. The artillery could not move forward as quickly as planned; the tanks bogged down unless they stuck to the roads; many of the infantry weapons became jammed with mud, and the Germans were remorseless in their counter-attacks. The initial optimism for a rapid advance started to fade away. As the days ticked by criticisms of Gough's methods began to mount, until at the end of August Haig eventually restricted the frontage for which he was responsible, and brought in Plumer to impose the strict organization and planning that had served him so well at Messines.

PLUMER TAKES OVER

At this point the rain stopped and the sun once again began to shine, but for the next three weeks the British were unable to exploit the dry

Passchendaele

weather. Plumer was reorganizing the assault forces, so the offensive was temporarily halted. It resumed on 20 September in grand style, with a succession of three textbook 'bite and hold' attacks, culminating at Broodseinde on 4 October. Of particular note was the inability of the German counter-attacks to make progress against the massive weight of British artillery fire. Whatever tactics the Germans attempted to employ, they appeared to be powerless in the face of this dominant arm. It was exactly how Haig's battle had been supposed to run in late June, and British spirits rose just as German optimism dissolved. However, it was now autumn moving into winter, and the rains began again, never to relent. In the long weeks after the heady success of Broodseinde the battlefield reverted to a heavily cratered bog, in which men could easily drown if they strayed away from the all too few duckboard paths. Depression and frustration set in as even the most normal operations became practically impossible. The Gheluvelt plateau was never totally captured, although the village of Passchendaele, at its summit, was captured by Canadian troops on 6 November, after which the whole operation was soon closed down. The allies had got nowhere near either Roulers or Ostend, and the cavalry Corps de Chasse had long ago been sent back to its stables.

The name 'Passchendaele' has entered the English language and consciousness as a symbol of the same type of futile sacrifice as was perceived to have occurred on the Somme a year earlier. However, in this case there were some added horrors which seemed to make the whole experience even worse. The most obvious was the rain and the all-pervasive mud, which the British public soon came to understand in a very vivid manner when the photographs were published after the war. The moonscape of shell craters filled with water, and devoid of all vegetation, made a very powerful impression. The very name 'Passchendaele' is itself resonant of squelching through deep, slimy mire.

Less well understood were some of the other horrors that were seen for the first time in this battle. Mustard gas was the first, and it was probably the nastiest gas of the entire war. The systematic use of concrete pillboxes by the Germans might be seen as another, in the

79

sense that they made it much harder than previously to knock out or neutralize an enemy machine gun post. A third horror, widely noted in the memoirs of participants, was what in modern parlance is called 'the deep battle', or the ability to reach deep behind enemy lines with firepower delivered by artillery and aircraft. Before Third Ypres the troops knew that they were almost totally safe from attack as soon as they had moved a couple of miles back from the front line. In the second half of 1917, however, this could no longer be relied upon. In particular the techniques of night bombing had become more advanced. Soldiers sleeping ten miles behind the front now found they were likely to be woken up, and perhaps even killed, by air raids. At the same time truly long-range artillery was available in ever increasing numbers and on the British side, at least, the science of first-round accuracy ('predicted fire') was being perfected for its use.

Many different sub-sciences had to be brought together before a gun could be relied upon to hit its target with its first shot. The weather had to be studied at every altitude through which the shell would travel. The firing characteristics of each individual gun had to be exactly known, especially since they were constantly changing as the barrel wore out. Each batch of shells was also subtly different from every other batch, and these differences had to be fully under-stood if their line of flight was to be predicted. Precise and detailed mapping was especially vital, to establish the locations of both the firing gun and its target. To achieve this it was necessary to set up a vast network of aircraft taking photographs of the terrain on a daily basis; laboratories to process and interpret the photographs; work-shops to convert the data into an accurately surveyed set of maps; and finally a printing and distribution system to get the maps to the guns and the tactical air photos to the infantry. During some operations new sets of maps and photographs had to be issued daily, as the situation on the ground kept changing. There was also a need for certain specialized techniques for locating enemy gun batteries, such as flash spotting or sound ranging. All this was enormously more sophisticated than anything that had been known before the war, and it amounted to a significant step forward in the 'art of war'.

Lord Kitchener of Khartoum recruiting his New Armies in 1914.

British troops conducting naively amateurish training in Scotland, 1914.

(Museum of Queen's Lancashire Regiment, Preston)

Too many French attacks in 1914 were defeated with heavy casualties when they failed to co-ordinate artillery support for their massed infantry. (***Illustrated War News** 7, 23 Sept. 1914*)

A light German field gun being manhandled into action, 1914.

(***Illustrated War News** 14, 11 Nov. 1914*)

The famous French 'soixante quinze' 75mm quick-firing field gun, which had revolutionized artillery in 1900 but was already too light for the needs of 1914.

Three British officers dining in their snug dugout.   (*Illustrated War News* 17, 2 Dec. 1914)

Indian troops at Fauquissart Post, Ypres area. Two Indian divisions were consumed on the Western Front in the winter of 1914-15, and not replaced.

Gurkhas with their fearsome kukris (fighting knives) near Neuve Chapelle in March 1915.

Soldiers with some of the new technology of trench warfare in the muzzles of their rifles, in the form of rifle grenades and wire cutters.

Chinese labourers at work on the British lines of communication: a vital but unsung resource.

French troops in the steep, stony and snowy terrain of the high Vosges.

Dragging up a big gun by hand, illustrating the poor mobility of artillery on the muddy battlefields of 1916.

Walking wounded British and German soldiers on the Somme, 1916.

'La Voie Sacrée' at Verdun in 1916: the vital road along which an endless column of motor lorries kept the garrison supplied.

The heroism of the trenches, 1916: this man was credited with rescuing twenty of his wounded comrades.

The small comforts of trench life, 1916: the 'Café Royal' canteen.

An infantry patrol crawling through wire and *chevaux de frise* around Beaumont Hamel, 1916.

President Poincaré and Marshal Joffre visit officers' quarters on the Somme, 1916.

Mining at Messines in 1916, in preparation for the battle in 1917. By this time the mine had been perfected as a technology for static warfare.

Training model of terrain at Messines, before the battle of June 1917. Careful briefing was a vital part of the 'rehearsal' phase in any battle.

A British advance in 1917, leaving typically shallow trenches.

A typical trench scene in 1917: British troops sleeping in mud holes.

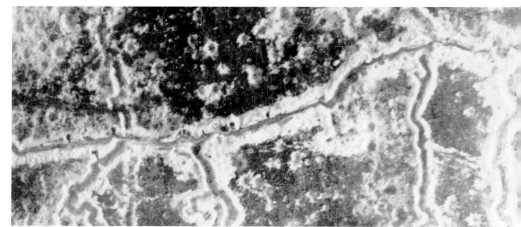

A classic view of the tortured moonscape of the Western Front, showing how clearly the trenches could be mapped from the air.

A forlorn plea to conserve ammunition, at a time when the British alone were firing off around a million shells per week.

Vickers machine gun engaged in long-range 'barrage' fire at Arras, 1917. This was an innovative technique for supplementing an artillery barrage.

ncient meets modern: airpower shares the battlefield with French cavalry whose sabres are rawn but whose carbines are slung.

anadians with a captured pillbox at Ypres, 1917. The Germans were at least a year ahead of the lies in the use of concrete for fortification.

erman troops in tactical pose at La Vacquerie, 1917.

US cemetery at Belleau Wood, where American troops halted the German Aisne offensive in June 1918.

US infantry at bayonet drill: an atavistic practice that was often mocked in this war of high explosives and advanced machinery.

General 'Black Jack' Pershing awarding congressional medals of honor at Chaumont, 1918.

3,000 of America's three million troops in France, 1918. This major new infusion of manpower would have been decisive if the war had continued into 1919.

A German machine gun team in the front line, 1918.

One of the very few German-built tanks, in September 1918. It was a mechanically execrable design.

A British Whippet (light and relatively fast) tank, during a muddy phase of the 'Hundred Days' in late 1918.

French 320mm railway guns in action, 1918. France was two years behind the central powers in the production of super-heavy artillery, but she caught up in the end.

The 'Strassenkampf', or civil war on the streets, in Berlin, late 1918.

Field Marshal Haig leading the British Empire troops in the Paris Victory March, 14 July 1919.

Passchendaele

Apart from anything else, the new artillery techniques meant that guns no longer needed to be pre-registered by the lengthy old methods of trial and error. In the past, this prolonged process had always given away the presence of the guns many days before an attack was launched, which in turn was a key intelligence indicator that an attack was imminent. An attacker was unable to achieve surprise, however well he might camouflage the build-up of his troops, so the defender had every opportunity to concentrate his reserves at the key point. With the new techniques of 'predicted fire', by contrast, the guns needed to support an attack could be kept hidden and silent right up to the moment when the infantry climbed out of its trenches and began its assault. The enemy could be kept in total ignorance of the impending offensive until about two minutes before it arrived on his forward positions.

This represented a revolution in tactics, which came to be understood by the British high command soon after the battle of Third Ypres had begun. Obviously by that stage it was already far too late to achieve surprise at Ypres itself, but General Byng, commanding the Third Army further to the south, realized that he had an ideal opportunity to do so on his frontage facing Cambrai. He devised a plan of attack, based around a surprise artillery bombardment using 'predicted fire'. Tanks were not originally part of this plan, as many have subsequently claimed, but they were added only later as an afterthought, to help crush the wire. The attack was carefully prepared in total secrecy during the first three weeks of November, and achieved total surprise when it was finally unleashed in the dawn mists of 20 November.

Despite the great strength of the Hindenburg Line defences, the assault troops rolled forward in splendid style. Most of the German artillery was knocked out almost instantly by accurate long-range fire; the wire was crushed under the tracks of some 378 tanks, and the infantry quickly occupied the enemy's front-line trenches. Only in front of Flesquières, in the second line of defence, did the attack encounter stiff resistance. The leading tanks had the misfortune to encounter a specialist battery that had been trained in anti-tank tactics, and were shot to pieces as they climbed up the slope. For all

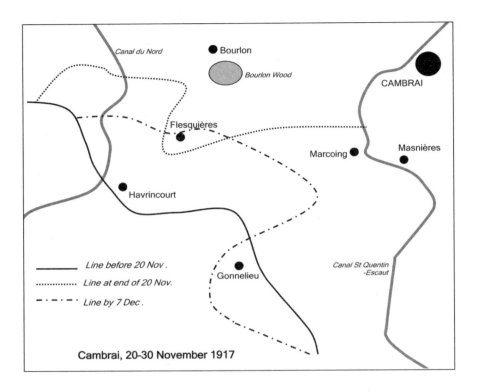

Cambrai, 20-30 November 1917

their strengths and shock value, Flesquières demonstrated that tanks were far from invulnerable to enemy fire, and in fact during the day as a whole no fewer than sixty-five were knocked out. A further 114 were immobilized by mechanical problems or bogging, so the attrition rate was running at around 50 per cent per day of combat. Another major problem was that the build-up of carbon monoxide and petrol fumes within each tank, especially when combined with motion sickness, severely limited the time its crew could continue in action. Six hours was a very good average; eight hours was absolutely heroic. When advancing carefully over a broken and complicated battlefield, this factor greatly restricted the distance a tank could advance in a day from its starting point, which would itself necessarily be some way behind the infantry's start line. In the case of

Passchendaele

Cambrai some tanks managed to advance as far as five miles into enemy territory on 20 November, but many more went much less far.

In the conditions of the Great War the tank could never possibly be considered a weapon of breakthrough. It had very limited range and speed, not to mention many other important tactical limitations. What it achieved at Cambrai was a great political triumph, in that at long last there were hundreds of tanks on the battlefield, rather than just a few dozens, and the progress made on 20 November was spectacular in the context of the Western Front. The church bells were rung in Britain upon receipt of the news, and the 'myth of the tank' entered the popular consciousness. The future of tank development and funding, which had been controversial ever since Bullecourt in April, was assured. The responsibility for making a breakthrough nevertheless remained firmly where it had always resided – with the horsed cavalry.

On 20 November it was the cavalry that was supposed to break through 'to the green fields beyond', and ultimately capture Cambrai itself. However the wide St Quentin Canal lay across the path of their intended advance, and by the time they got there only one rickety bridge remained. Some of the cavalry got across and established a bridgehead; but the whole impetus of their forward charge had been wrecked. The Germans were granted time to bring up reinforcements and make a fight of it after all. This meant that the successes of the first day, which had certainly been great, would lead to no breakthrough but only a new round of attritional trench warfare. It became focused on Bourlon Wood, a hill feature overlooking the whole battlefield from the north. The British finally took it on 23 November, only to lose it again on the 27th. At this stage of the battle Byng had run out of reserves, since his operation had only ever been conceived on a relatively small scale when compared with the major offensive that had just finished at Ypres. Indeed, he now found he had perilously few troops left to defend the ground he had won.

The Germans duly exploited the British weakness by mounting two major counter-attacks on 30 November, of which the one towards the south-east flank of the British salient was particularly effective. Much of the ground captured on the 20th was retaken and the balance of casualties, which had previously been heavily in favour of the British, was restored almost to equality. For the British it made a disappointing end to a battle that had started so well. For the Germans it demonstrated that in favourable circumstances they could still land well-prepared offensive blows with infantry spearheads following a hurricane bombardment. At Ypres the British artillery had been too strong and the terrain too broken for this tactic to work; but at Cambrai it worked well and pointed the way to a series of successful offensives in spring 1918. Nevertheless, the overall result at Cambrai was something of a drawn match. The breakthrough that had eluded tacticians in 1916 thus continued to elude them right to the end of 1917.

CHAPTER SEVEN

The Bitter Winter of 1917–18

The Bitter Winter of 1917–18

The war was changing in nature over the winter of 1917–18. In France a new impetus towards victory was imparted by Georges Clemenceau, 'the Tiger', when he became prime minister in November at the age of seventy-six. He took semi-dictatorial powers into the hands of government and made great efforts to combat defeatism among soldiers and civilians alike. He famously said that 'war is too important to be left to the generals', although in practice he would do much to smooth the path for his military commanders. In particular he backed the claims of General Ferdinand Foch to become supreme commander on the Western Front, which would add a long overdue rationality to the chain of command during the dangerous days of March.

As for the British, they had suffered something like a quarter of a million casualties at Third Ypres, and a further 50,000 at Cambrai. The army was exhausted and oppressed. At home, Prime Minister Lloyd George was appalled on two counts. The first was the obvious dislike for heavy casualties that any humane person ought to feel, but the second was of considerably greater importance to him. This was his frustration that in political terms Haig was more powerful than he was himself. The army stood behind Haig, and so he could not be sacked at the height of such a major war. Haig's policy was to continue to concentrate maximum resources on the Western Front, the most important theatre facing the most important enemy. But this meant that Lloyd George had no choice but to agree. He had very little of the 'wriggle room' that is always so dear to politicians in general, and to this one in particular.

Throughout the war the civilian Lloyd George, along with Churchill, had made a habit of trying to outflank the professional military men. In 1915 both of them were already looking to campaigns in the Dardanelles, Salonika and Palestine as alternatives to a war of attrition on the Western Front. Then they accelerated the procurement of tanks as an alternative to sacrificial infantry attacks, while unreasonably blaming General Headquarters (GHQ) in France for dragging its feet. Lloyd George also accused the generals of failing to realize the importance of machine guns, just as he accused the admirals of failing to adopt the convoy system. By 1917 he seemed to reckon himself something of a military expert, while continuing to support the 'eastern' theatres against the Western Front. These now included sending troops from France to the Italian front, and exaggerating the achievements of the nascent Arab Revolt. Especially in 1919–20 the champions of eastern policies would make a point of lionizing T E Lawrence 'of Arabia', in his flowing white robes, as a totally alternative figure to any of the dour khaki-clad generals from GHQ who had actually won the war.

By the start of 1918 Lloyd George was thus already trying his best to find some wriggle room to undermine Haig's 'western' policy. He now went two steps further: first by getting some of Haig's top staff officers sacked, most notably his chief of intelligence, John Charteris. More important, he exacerbated the existing recruitment crisis by holding back many thousands of reinforcements in Britain, thereby forcing a radical reduction in the fighting strength of the BEF on the Western Front. This was doubly unfortunate because it came at a moment when the British had to take over a further twenty-five miles of front line from the French. In effect they were being told to reduce their manpower per mile of front by about half, and nowhere more so than at the southern end of their line, where Gough's Fifth Army was taking over the positions opposite St Quentin that the French were evacuating.

That in itself might have been acceptable if the British had been posted on a 'quiet sector'. After the many massive blows they had landed on the Germans ever since 31 July 1917, they had some justification for thinking that the enemy opposite them should have been reduced to quiescence. Even if not, by this point in the war both Lloyd George and Haig had come to assume that the defence would always be far more powerful than any attack, at least after the attacker had been able to make a significant advance on his carefully prepared 'first day'. There was a certain complacency that even at half strength, a defender could always hold out for long enough to allow reinforcements to arrive and plug any gaps in the line. Why, even the ferocious German counter-attack at Cambrai had eventually

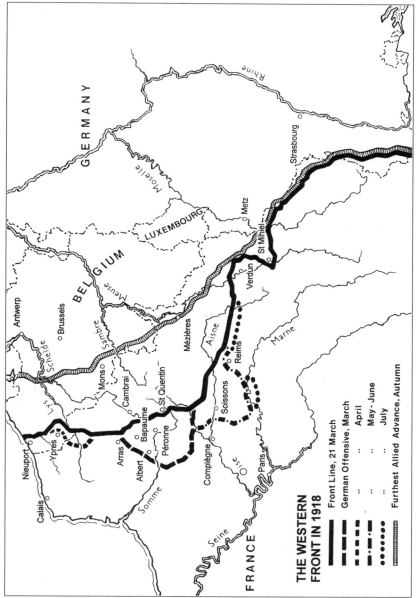

THE WESTERN
FRONT IN 1918

	Front Line, 21 March
	German Offensive, March
	" " " April
	" " " May – June
	" " " July
	Furthest Allied Advance, Autumn

Map drawn by Ed Dovey.

89

been held without any very seriously dramatic loss of territory, had it not?

Alas for these expectations, the whole German situation was changing over the winter of 1917–18. The Russians had finally been knocked out of the war with an armistice on 3 December, thereby releasing some forty-four divisions from the German armies in the East to be transferred to the West. Ludendorff massed them between Cambrai and St Quentin to launch a major offensive on 21 March, with nineteen divisions to attack Byng's fourteen divisions of Third Army (holding a 28-mile front), and no fewer than forty-three divisions to attack Gough's twelve divisions of Fifth Army (holding a 42-mile front). Also of great importance was the fact that they brought with them some new tactics from the East.

Often called 'stormtroop tactics' or 'Hutier tactics', these eastern methods consisted of a number of properly distinct elements. The first was an attempt to achieve operational surprise up to the moment when the bombardment started, by all possible methods of camouflage, deception and security. Second, there would be a hurricane bombardment carefully orchestrated by the rising star and showman of the German artillery, Colonel Georg Bruchmüller. He was pushing forward with the arts of 'predicted fire' that the British had already perfected, although for a long time he was better at getting a good line rather than good length with any given shell. He also encountered scepticism from his colleagues, so his preliminary bombardments would typically represent something of a compromise, starting more or less six hours before the infantry attack began, rather than simultaneously with it. During those six hours his guns would fire at the fastest rate, scouring backwards and forwards over all the enemy positions within range and particularly, in the absence of fully reliable 'first round accuracy', firing gas shell as an area weapon to neutralize his gun pits. Bruchmüller, whose nickname was 'Durchbruchmüller' (or 'Breakthrough Müller'), had used this mixture at Riga in September 1917 to excellent effect.

When the infantry attacked they would be spearheaded by 'stormtroops' (originally specialist assault pioneers) trained to use all types of infantry assault weapons in the same way that Laffargue had

The Bitter Winter of 1917–18

understood in 1915, and the British had incorporated into their manual of February 1917. Within each company there would be portable machine guns, trench mortars, flamethrowers and light trench guns. These were not really innovative tactics, as has often been claimed, but Ludendorff broke with the earlier German practice of leaving them to specialists, by attempting to teach them to the majority of his army over the winter of 1917–18. Like Bruchmüller's bombardments, they had been successfully tested in combat by General Oskar von Hutier at Riga, and he too was called to France to participate in the March offensives. In the event Riga turned out to have been the last battle fought against the Russians and, as such, the Germans were facing an already half-defeated enemy whose positions were rather widely dispersed. The leading spearheads of assaulting infantry were able to infiltrate between and behind them, often capturing them without serious fighting, in a way that would not have been possible against the dense fortifications of the Western Front in 1916–17. Unfortunately for the British, however, the conditions at Riga were exactly the same as would obtain in Gough's Fifth Army near St Quentin on 21 March 1918.

It was bad enough that Gough's men were battle-weary, understrength, overstretched on a frontage too long for their numbers, and badly outnumbered. It was much worse that they were badly deployed. For three months before the enemy attacked they had been under orders to imitate the German methods of depth defence, which meant a very lightly held front line backed by stronger positions in the second and third lines. In practice, however, the main bulk of the Fifth Army forces remained in the front line, on the reasoning that there were not enough men to occupy the two rearward lines, which in any case had not yet been built. This left them very vulnerable to the initial German bombardment and assault. Gough's personal reputation must stand or fall on the question of whether he could possibly have done anything to correct these arrangements, and there are indeed some extenuating circumstances. For example, he was unlucky that there was thick morning mist shrouding most of his battlefield at the moment the enemy attacked, and it was noted that the defence was much more successful at the points that were clear of mist. On the balance of probability, however, it seems likely that he must personally shoulder considerable blame.

The Germans encountered a properly consolidated defence on the front of Byng's Third Army, north of the Fifth Army, and they were duly beaten off in no uncertain manner, just as they would doubtless have been on most other sections of the old, settled and well organized Western Front. On Gough's front, by contrast, once they had shattered the front line, they were able to infiltrate through it in all directions. In the second and third British lines they encountered no continuous front, but only scattered strongpoints or improvised groupings of retreating troops who could usually be outflanked. When the German spearheads began to start such an outflanking movement, the defenders would have a choice between holding their ground and being surrounded, or retreating to the next defensible position in the hope that the attackers would finally run out of steam. Normally it was the second option that was preferred, which meant that the increasingly notional 'British front line' kept on moving to the rear, and the whole cycle would start over again.

The German spearheads kept on surging forward, hustling Gough's troops out of the way, for an astounding forty miles in the space of just a week. This was an advance that beat the British achievement at Cambrai some eight times over, even without the help of tanks, and it was surely the nearest thing to a 'breakthrough' that had yet been seen on the Western Front. However, the further they advanced, the more the German troops became exhausted and exposed to increasingly effective attacks from a once again dominant and increasingly sophisticated allied air force.[1] Some British ground attack pilots reported 'cricket match crowds' marching down roads behind the front line, where they could be mown down in droves. Thus the high tactical training of the successful German front-line troops did not apparently extend to their whole army, whose overall losses mounted inexorably.

The advancing Germans also became separated not only from their artillery, but especially from their rations. They took to looting, and were amazed to find that the lavish scale of food and wine enjoyed by their opponents was greatly superior to their own. By this stage in the war the allied blockade of Germany was cutting deep, and it was still too early to expect grain from Russia and the Ukraine to arrive to alleviate the situation. The contrast between the nutritional provision of the two sides was striking, and it was not lost on Ludendorff's legions. The seeds of depression, war weariness and even combat refusal began to germinate within their ranks.

The offensive was finally halted on 5 April, two weeks after the 'first day', at Villers-Bretonneux, some ten miles short of Amiens. This was the apex of the new German salient, whose southern flank ran all the way back to Noyon. During the two weeks of the battle each side had suffered around a quarter of a million casualties, which rather mocked Lloyd George's notion that he could reduce losses if he forced Haig onto the defensive by giving him inadequate numbers. And apart from the physical losses, there had understandably been something approaching panic at every level in the allied ranks. The troops of Gough's army normally walked to the rear in good order, and rarely ran. Nevertheless, their daily marches were often long and bewildering. There was vast confusion and administrative chaos, as HQs had to move unexpectedly from one location to another, and phone lines were constantly cut. Units became detached or lost, and had to be reunited with their parent formations. In the long run all this provided HQ staffs with some splendid training in mobile warfare that would serve them in good stead during the autumn offensives. In the short term, however, it merely added to their problems.

At the highest echelons of command the generals had all been taken by surprise by the rapidity and extent of German success. At first Haig's instinct was to call in French and American reinforcements from the south towards the BEF; conversely, Pétain was anxious to consolidate his own positions, especially to cover Paris, and was reluctant to release any more reserves than had previously been promised. General John 'Black Jack' Pershing, commander of the ever growing American Expeditionary Force (AEF), had been insisting for the previous nine months that he would not allow his forces to join the battle piecemeal, but only after they had been built up to full strength and formed into a consolidated all-American army. It caused the three allied powers considerable heartache to get their act together, but at a conference on 26 March at Doullens, north of Amiens, they finally reached an agreement. General Ferdinand Foch was appointed as 'Generalissimo' (later given the formal title of Commander-in-Chief) of all the allied armies in France (later extended to other theatres as well) – a single authority who could impose some sort of higher operational coherence upon the competing allied contingents. Lloyd George was delighted that this at long last brought Haig under a higher command; Haig himself, though, was equally delighted that at last there was someone who could prod the pessimistic Pétain into a greater show of inter-allied solidarity. As for Pershing, by this time he had already agreed to release some of his troops to help out, although his combat-ready total was still scarcely more than six divisions. The first American attack would be mounted by 1st Division at Cantigny, at the tip of the German salient on the Somme, on 28 May.

Thus it was that a long-overdue allied unity emerged out of the shock of 21 March, and major French reserves were moved north to the area of Amiens, rather than retreating southwards towards Paris. By the time they arrived in position, however, the German offensive had fizzled out at Villers-Bretonneux, where a variety of allied second-echelon troops, including some US and British engineers, were able to hold the line against the final German push.[2] Villers-Bretonneux itself would continue to be the scene of some technically advanced fighting, notably the very first tank versus tank combat on 24 April, when three of the very few German tanks were defeated by three British tanks. Then on 4 July the village of Hamel, just to the east, was captured in a model surprise attack by Australian troops with some US support. Finally, this whole area would be the scene of the great 'battle of Amiens' on 8 August, in which the lessons of Hamel were reapplied on a much greater scale and with much greater results.

THE GERMAN OFFENSIVES CONTINUE

By the end of March Ludendorff had already begun to redirect his reserves, and Bruchmüller's artillery train, further to the north. On 9 April, the first anniversary of the battle of Arras, he launched a new

The Bitter Winter of 1917–18

offensive in the area of the Lys, following a thirty-six-hour bombardment. His first offensive from St Quentin had carried the Germans back over the old battlefields of the Somme, but now the tide of war flowed again over the old British battlefields of 1915 between Neuve Chapelle and Armentières, and over the 1917 killing grounds at Passchendaele itself, as well as Messines and Kemmel just south of Ypres. On this occasion, however, the shock was less than in March and the defence better organized. The two Portuguese divisions exposed in the front line were quickly crushed, but German progress was slow. French and other allied reinforcements eventually arrived to support an orderly British withdrawal. At around ten miles, the total depth of the German penetration was still impressive by the normal standards of 1915–17, but it soon became clear that this would not be the runaway drive to the Channel ports that Haig had most feared. It was finally halted some five miles short of the intended target, the rail junction at Hazebrouck, and degenerated into positional warfare that finally petered out at the end of the month. The German casualties were almost 100,000 – unusually, nearly twice those of the allies. Ludendorff had missed his chance to make a rapid exploitation of his victory on the Somme in March. He was also demonstrating a certain randomness in his ideas, thrashing around from one direction of attack to another, instead of concentrating upon a single *Schwerpunkt*.

There was a pause following the end of the battle of the Lys, but on 27 May Ludendorff lunged again in a completely different direction. He hit the French just north of the Chemin des Dames, where they had come to rest after the Nivelle Offensive of spring 1917. This time Bruchmüller's preliminary bombardment lasted only three hours, and surprise was achieved by an assault of seventeen German divisions against an allied front line manned by only four French and three British divisions. The stubbornly outdated tactics of the French Sixth Army commander, General Denis Auguste Duchêne, dictated that the defences were all bunched too far to the front, and they had two rivers too close behind them. All intelligence of the impending offensive had also been brushed aside, sealing the doom of the defenders. The British were particularly unfortunate, since they had

The Great War on the Western Front

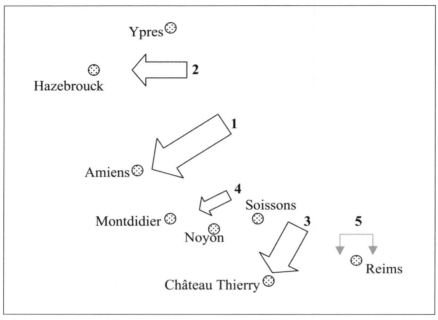

The five German offensives of 1918: (1) St Quentin, 21 March; (2) Lys, 9 April; (3) Aisne, 27 May; (4) Noyon-Montdidier, 9 June; and (5) Reims, 15 July.

been moved to this 'quiet sector' after being battered first in the March offensive and then again in April. Now, although they were very well aware of what was about to happen, they were powerless to change General Duchêne's dispositions and were battered once again. The Germans advanced twelve miles in the first day, crossing not only the steep ridge of the Chemin des Dames, but also the river Aisne itself. The French reserves were bundled away to the rear, and the next day the Germans crossed the river Vesle as well. In his original plan Ludendorff had intended to halt at that, and redirect his reserves back to Flanders, but the heady scent of victory persuaded him to press on instead to Paris, which now seemed to be within reach. In three days the Germans reached the north bank of the Marne at Château Thierry, some thirty-five miles beyond their starting line. The apex of their new salient was in Belleau Wood, about four miles to the west of Château Thierry, while its north-easternmost point was at Noyon.

At that point the whirlwind advance was finally halted in early June, partly by the arrival of two American divisions who beat off all attacks on both sides of the river, and partly by Pétain's careful organization of other reinforcements. In part, however, the German spearheads were slowed down not only by superior allied air power, but also by just the same type of looting as had hindered them on the Somme two months earlier. This was, after all, the Champagne region!

German problems were increased when the US 2nd Division counter-attacked Belleau Wood on 6 June. At first their tactical methods were naive and costly, but they gradually learned better ways and the wood was finally cleared almost a month later. The capture of the village of Vaux on 1 July was a particularly slick and well-planned success. Overall the Aisne offensive had cost both sides about 125,000 casualties. The allies had received a rude shock and General Duchêne, just like Gough before him, was justly dismissed from his post. Yet on the German side Ludendorff found that by failing to halt his advance on the Vesle, he had bitten off more than he could chew. His front line in the new salient was too far forward, and its length was about twice as long as he had planned. He now abandoned his aim of switching his effort back to Flanders, and instead opted to site his next offensive between the salient achieved in March and the new one of May. If he could straighten the line between the two, he would have an excellent baseline for a concerted attack on Paris.

The Noyon-Montdidier offensive, the fourth in quick succession, was launched southwards from the area won in March. It began on 9 June, once again led by the team of Hutier and Bruchmüller. On this occasion, however, they achieved no operational surprise because the French high command could read the map just as well as Ludendorff, and they had correctly predicted where his next thrust would come. French artillery was already putting down fire on the German front lines before Bruchmüller revealed his hand. Even so the assault gained seven miles on the first day, and crossed the river Matz on the second. Yet Pétain had shrewdly positioned his reserves so that even when the front line of divisions had been overwhelmed, the second line was not. Indeed, General Mangin actually counter-attacked on the third day with some three French and two American divisions, including tanks. All this stopped the Germans dead in their tracks, and Ludendorff abandoned his offensive on the fifth day, 13 June. If he had been wise he would have gone back to the defensive at once, to husband his reserves. But because he was a gambler by nature, he chose to roll the dice yet again.

In his Aisne offensive in May Ludendorff had hoped to draw the allied reserves to the south, so that he could then return quickly to Flanders and finally throw the British into the sea. But the runaway success of the Aisne attack had distracted him with the prospect of capturing Paris, and this chimera continued to motivate him in the Noyon-Montdidier attack. However, the relative failure of the latter operation led him to think again about Flanders. He reverted to his late May logic, whereby threatening Paris, from anywhere around the Aisne or the Marne, would necessarily bring the allied reserves scurrying to the south, leaving the British in Flanders vulnerable to a final decisive hammer blow that would knock them out of the war.

There was an unfortunate month's delay before the fifth German offensive was launched, to east and west of Reims, on 15 July. It was heralded as the 'peace offensive' (*Friedensturm*), or the final battle that would simultaneously win and end the war in a single blow. This represented precisely the same psychological mistake that Nivelle had made in his offensive of April 1917: it raised the hopes of the troops far too high before the battle, only to dash them down into despair later, once it had become obvious that the war had not actually ended. In this case the disillusionment came for Ludendorff's armies even faster than it had for Nivelle's. The offensive was also heralded to the allies, who were able to see through the German preparations far more accurately on this occasion than they had in the previous four assaults.

The heady successes of 21 March and 27 May would not be re-peated on the Marne in July, and it was soon clear that Ludendorff's forward impetus was faltering. To the east of Reims General Henri

The Bitter Winter of 1917–18

Gouraud applied an even more effective defence in depth than had been used to resist the Noyon-Montdidier offensive, let alone by the scornful Duchêne on the Chemin des Dames, or by Gough at St Quentin. On Gouraud's front the Germans attacked with storm-troops and twenty tanks, but they were brought to a halt as early as the morning of the first day. Bruchmüller was decisively defeated for the first time in his life, and the French art of defence finally came of age, about a year after their post-Nivelle art of attack had done so.

To the south-west of Reims the Germans made rather better progress and succeeded in making a textbook assault river crossing over the Marne to the east of Château Thierry. They carved out a bridge-head four miles deep on a frontage of nine miles, but by 17 July they had been halted there as completely as they had been by Gouraud to the east. Ludendorff was anxious not to let his men advance too far, and in any case he had already sent off Bruchmüller's guns to Flanders. But worse was to come. The following day the French mounted a large-scale counter-offensive into the whole Château Thierry salient from the south and east, thereby threatening the latest Marne crossings in the rear. Surprise was achieved by marching the assault troops into position only at the very last moment, and excel-lent initial progress was made against sparse enemy defences.

There had been a variety of small or relatively small counter-attacks against some of the earlier German thrusts, but none had been as big or as significant as this one. It included some seventeen French and US divisions, 346 Renault light tanks and some horsed cavalry. Although few of the tanks remained in running order at the end of the first day, and the cavalry was cut down in a matter of minutes, the infantry continued to make good progress into the salient until the Germans managed to consolidate their defences. Ludendorff eventually organized an orderly withdrawal from the southern tip of his salient, but he lost some 30,000 prisoners, and could not resist the incessant pressure from south and west. The key rail junction at Soissons was liberated on 2 August, although by then the offensive was running to a standstill along the line of the Vesle. It was finally called off altogether on 6 August, after regaining much of the ground lost since 27 May. This was the same day that Foch was promoted to be a marshal of France.[3]

The German attack and the Franco-American counter-attack are collectively known as the second battle of the Marne. Overall it cost some 130,000 allied and 200,000 German casualties, which at least showed a certain actuarial advantage to the allies. It also brought the German total of casualties since 21 March to a staggering total of one million (of whom 124,000 were killed, as against 67,000 killed from Britain and 220,000 from France). Of greater significance, however, was the fact that the French had launched the first major counter-attack in what would quickly become an ever-expanding hail of similar blows, along the whole length of the Western Front. It also marked the end of Ludendorff's offensives. His long-planned attack in Flanders was cancelled and his forces reverted to the defensive for the remainder of the war. After four months of desperate fighting, the tide had finally turned.

CHAPTER EIGHT

The Flashing Sword of the Counter-Offensive

The Flashing Sword of the Counter-Offensive

The second battle of the Marne was brought to an end only two days before the next allied attack was launched, at Amiens on 8 August. This time it was a joint Anglo-French enterprise, with the British taking the lead after three months' licking their wounds and sending reinforcements to the French as required. Amiens was their first major deliberate offensive since Cambrai eight months earlier, but they had forgotten none of their art of attack during the intervening time. All the careful planning, deception, camouflage and secrecy that had gone into preparing the raid on Cambrai was also bestowed on the 'first day' at Amiens, although on this occasion with much stronger reserves close at hand, and a much weaker enemy defensive system to attack. Only at zero hour did 2,000 guns open fire, using a mixture of pre-registered and predicted fire. Some 324 heavy tanks accompanied the initial assault, with a further 200 tracked armoured vehicles, of various types, in reserve. There was also a technically sophisticated Corps de Chasse waiting behind the lines to exploit early success with horsed cavalry, machine guns mounted on motor cycles, armoured cars and ninety-six Whippet fast tanks. Large-scale air operations were co-ordinated with the attack, first to drown out the noise of tank movements during the assembly phase, and then to conduct intensive ground attack against the enemy's troops in and just behind his defensive lines, and to destroy the Somme bridges in his rear. Of particular interest were the plans for close liaison between the RAF and the Corps de Chasse in the breakout phase. This was surely the direction in which mobile operations would evolve not only during the remainder of 1918, but also through all the remainder of military history.

The troops of Rawlinson's Fourth Army went over the top on 8 August in a thick fog which greatly assisted their attack, even if it hindered all their supporting air operations. They consisted of (from south to north) one army corps each of Canadians, Australians and British. They enjoyed success in that order, with the Canadians on the right winning the most ground, and the British doing least well. Indeed, their relative failure provoked a new burst of the now-routine

The Great War on the Western Front

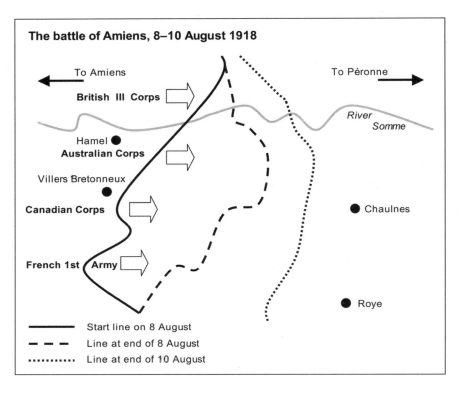

The battle of Amiens, 8–10 August 1918

To Amiens

British III Corps

To Péronne

River *Somme*

Hamel ●
Australian Corps

Villers Bretonneux ●

Canadian Corps

● Chaulnes

French 1st Army

● Roye

——————— Start line on 8 August
– – – Line at end of 8 August
············· Line at end of 10 August

ANZAC fury against the imperial power, this time because it was claimed that the British failed to secure the Australians' left flank in the later stages of their advance. On the Canadians' right flank, by contrast, there was a generally successful attack by the French First Army, which prevented enemy intervention from that direction.

It was also on the Canadian sector that the Corps de Chasse went through and created considerable mayhem in the enemy's rear. It did not manage to achieve a technical 'breakthrough', but it certainly earned its pay in a way that previous attempts to exploit an initial infantry 'break-in' had signally failed to do. It captured a rich harvest of prisoners and guns, and pushed the front line still further forward than the infantry and heavy tanks had advanced, to a total of about seven miles from the start line. Significantly, the horsed cavalry caused distinctly greater damage to the enemy than the Whippet tanks, and surely no less than the armoured cars. One cavalry regiment even captured an entire train full of enemy soldiers. For all that, it was the mass of (ill-distinguished) tanks that weighed most heavily upon German minds, especially since the deployment of a total of over 600 tanks at Amiens came so soon after the French had used 346 tanks in their Soissons offensive. The total was about 1,000 in all, which contrasted vividly with the poor twenty (including six captured from the British) that the Germans had deployed against Gouraud on 15 July. In 1937 General Heinz Guderian would write his seminal book *Achtung Panzer!*, which dwelt at length upon precisely this disparity and called – with, alas, only too much success – for the German army to be equipped as a matter of urgency with a large and effective Panzer arm.

The late summer of 1918 also marked the first time since the Somme in 1916 when the side that was winning on the ground was also winning in the air. In 1917 the Germans had been on the defensive but had often enjoyed local air superiority, while in the spring of 1918 they had been rampant on the ground but constrained by bigger and better allied air forces. Now at last those air forces were free to support a major allied offensive on the ground, which allowed them to develop a number of new roles and tactics that would soon become standard practice for every air force. One was to drop ammunition to forward troops who had outrun their logistics by the very speed of their advance, which happened on a small scale on 8 August. This pointed the way forward to many much larger air resupply operations during the remainder of the twentieth century, not least the Berlin Air Lift of 1948–9. The battle of Amiens also saw a major attempt at 'battlefield interdiction' designed to destroy bridges just behind the enemy fighting line, to stop the flow of his supplies and reinforcements. On this occasion it was not successful, and a total of ninety-six RAF aircraft were lost while trying to cut the Somme bridges around Péronne, but it nevertheless remained a pointer for the future use of air power.

The loss of ninety-six aircraft on a single mission was certainly exceptional, but even without that, in most months of the Great War there was more than a 65 per cent loss of front-line aircraft to all causes, although only some 7 per cent in combat. In other words a fighting air force of 600 machines could expect to lose an average of 390 within thirty days, or thirteen per day, which implied that production had to run at some 4,680 per year if full strength were to be maintained. In the circumstances of 1914–18 this placed an incredible strain upon the industrial resources of the state, especially in the mass production of high-performance engines, which was a science that was still in its infancy.[1]

The Germans did not totally disintegrate in the battle of Amiens, although they came very close to doing so. Mutinous shouts and graffiti were encountered in their rear echelons, which added a newly ominous undertone to what was already a dramatic loss of territory, armaments and men. The promises made in July that the Reims offensive would end the war in a day were rebounding badly on the high command. Ludendorff called 8 August 'the black day of the German army', and in his mind, as well as in the minds of many of his generals, it conclusively reinforced the main lesson of the Franco-American success at Soissons earlier the same week. Nor did subsequent events help to calm him down. Although German reinforcements were already arriving in force during the following day, the allies were able to make a new advance of about half as far as they had on 8 August, and on the day after that it was still about a quarter as far. The French also widened the front further to the south, and recaptured Montdidier. On the other hand, the tank strength available to the allies was more or less halved on each of these days until it wasted away to almost nothing, exactly as it had done during the first few days of both Cambrai and the French Soissons counter-offensive. All three of these battles confirmed the very short combat life of a fighting tank, and therefore its unsuitability as a weapon of breakout.

On 11 August, the fourth day at Amiens, the British closed down their offensive, following the wise maxim of the French General Marie Fayolle that 'after the third day, an offensive is just a waste'. Marshal Foch, who always wanted any attack to be pressed on and on to its bitterest end, was furious. He was no friend of the 'bite and hold' mentality. Yet this was exactly the same day that Ludendorff

The Flashing Sword of the Counter-Offensive

offered his resignation to the Kaiser, who refused to accept it but decided nevertheless that the war was lost. Nor was he wrong, since there were many other allied forces waiting to take over the baton from the temporarily stalled British Fourth Army. Each of them in turn was ready to bite and then hold in its own time, regardless of whatever Foch might think. At least the overall effect would soon add up to something very much like a 'general offensive along the whole front', which is surely what Foch really wanted to see, even if he may not have been entirely clear about it in his own mind.

The casualties at Amiens finally totalled about 75,000 Germans, 22,000 from the BEF and 24,000 French, although it was doubtless more significant that the rude shock to the Germans' morale was just as great as the corresponding boost to the allies'. Yet the high casualties from just four days' fighting were an ominous pointer to the future. During the next 'Hundred Days' of allied offensives the losses to all participating forces would continue to run very high indeed, despite the undoubted shift of the initiative – and the ultimate victory – to the allies. No battle on the Western Front would ever have a small 'butcher's bill', even when the enemy was on the run or, as in this case, merely waiting for the war to end.

The next attack after Amiens was launched on 21 August by Byng's Third Army on the northern end of the old Somme battlefield, and by General Henry Horne's First Army even further to the north. Meanwhile the French were resuming their attacks all the way south from the Amiens battlefield to Noyon. There was success everywhere, and Byng's inexperienced young troops won a particularly notable victory on 22 August when, instead of pressing their attack, they held the ground won the previous day and shot down a series of counter-attacks, thereby making it all the easier to resume their advance on the 23rd. That day, 22 August, was also the day on which Rawlinson's Fourth Army recaptured Albert. The whole front was shaking itself down, rising from its trenches and moving eastwards in a slow, methodical but nonetheless insistent manner.

In the First Army's battle of the Scarpe on 26–28 August the Canadian corps pushed forward some six miles over the parts of the old Arras battlefield that had not been captured in April 1917.

The Great War on the Western Front

Meanwhile Byng's army was advancing on either side of Bapaume, capturing the town on the night of 28–29 August, and the Australians in the Fourth Army were reaching towards Péronne. Ludendorff had ordered the construction of a 'Winter Line' in that area, based on the south–north section of the Somme river up to Péronne, and its northerly extension along the Canal du Nord. As the name suggests, his hope was that he would be able to consolidate his army in this strong position, hold out through September, and then sit back over the remainder of the winter while the weather closed down further allied offensives.

As early as 1 September, however, Monash and his Australians had blown the German plan to smithereens by one of the most notable *actions d'éclat* of the entire war. In a three-day battle, and without either a creeping barrage or tanks, they crossed three trench lines and seized the linchpin of Ludendorff's whole system at Mont St Quentin, just north of Péronne. The 'Winter Line' had to be hastily abandoned and Ludendorff was forced to think instead in terms of holding out on the main Hindenburg position along the St Quentin Canal, some seventeen miles further to the east. Unlike the 'Winter Line', these fortifications had existed for over eighteen months and were formidably deep. There was much discussion in both GHQ and the war cabinet over the question of whether it would be sensible to attack them at all, especially since so much of the BEF was either exhausted by repeated battles since 21 March, or inexperienced boys fresh from home. At some points in the debate it looked as though Ludendorff would get his way and be allowed to ride out the winter without coming under serious attack.

The Canadians, ably supported by some British divisions, went some way to answering GHQ's doubts on 2 September when they won a particularly brisk success by penetrating the Drocourt-Quéant line some ten miles south-east of Arras. Strictly speaking this was already a part of the Hindenburg system, with wire barriers up to 100 yards deep. To that extent the Canadians had already demonstrated that it could be breached, some three weeks before the Third and Fourth Armies came up against the 'main' part of it north of St Quentin. During the first of these weeks Ludendorff performed a

The Flashing Sword of the Counter-Offensive

general step back by all his armies from the ground they had won in the spring, including in Flanders. On many occasions there were scenes reminiscent of the original step back to the Hindenburg Line in February and March 1917, as the pursuit plugged on forward. Then in the second week the defence firmed up and the approaches to the Hindenburg Line had to be cleared in a series of local attacks, such as at Epéhy on 18 September. Meanwhile the logistic preparations for the great assault were begun.

On the Franco-American front there was an attack to clear the St Mihiel salient on 12 September. It was entirely successful because the German commander had read the allied plans in the newspapers, and had begun to evacuate the salient about twelve hours before the attack began. Most of the bombardment by 3,000 guns therefore fell on empty space, but this did not delay the rapid advance, and the whole salient was cleared within twenty-five hours, with 14,500 prisoners captured for the very light cost of 8,000 allied casualties. There had been an acrimonious argument between Pershing, Foch and Haig over where the Americans should go next, but in the end it had been agreed that they should drive north through the Argonne forest towards Mézières, rather than north-east to Metz. Haig had urged this decision upon his allies because it represented a line of advance that was more convergent with the direction being taken by the BEF.

The Americans were to begin their attack on 26 September, after which the British First and Third armies would strike towards Cambrai, then the Second Army eastwards from Ypres and finally, on the 29th, Rawlinson's Fourth Army would make its carefully prepared frontal assault to break the Hindenburg Line (Siegfried position) north of St Quentin. Meanwhile the French were preparing their own advances in step with the general offensive, south of St Quentin and on the Aisne and Champagne fronts. They were of course perfectly happy to allow their allies to shoulder the main weight of the fighting at this stage in the war, since they could not forget the first two years on the Western Front, when the British had to all intents and purposes fought to the last Frenchman.

The Great War on the Western Front

We will return to the Americans in the next chapter; for the moment suffice it to say that both the Cambrai and the Ypres attacks went like clockwork. The first took less than a day to capture Bourlon and its wood, which had eluded Byng in his offensive of November 1917. This effectively outflanked the Siegfried position from the north, thereby greatly increasing the uncertainties in the minds of its defenders facing the Fourth Army nearer to St Quentin. Cambrai itself would fall on 8 October. In Flanders the triumph was if anything even sweeter, since almost the whole of the Gheluvelt plateau fell to Plumer's men in a day, whereas in the previous year it had defied them for four long and blood-soaked months. By 2 October the attack was finally knocking at the gates of both Roulers and Menin, which in 1917 had existed as objectives in the minds of Haig and his GHQ staff, but which in the minds of the front-line troops had seemed to be rather further away than the moon.

FROM THE HINDENBURG LINE TO THE ARMISTICE

The big test, and the crunch point upon which Haig's whole offensive would either prosper or collapse, was the attack on the Siegfried position on 29 September. In the 'semi-mobile warfare' of the Hundred Days that started on 8 August, few of the British attacks had been preceded by a well-prepared bombardment, let alone a long one. Occasionally there had been predicted fire; more usually there had not. Sometimes there had been a creeping barrage; sometimes not. Six hours was probably about the longest preliminary bombardment that had been seen, certainly nothing like the week-long or two-week bombardments of 1916 and 1917. On the other hand most of the attacks had been launched against ill-prepared fortifications, mostly built in the spring by German troops at the end of long and exhausting offensives, at a moment when defence was the very last thing on their minds. Even if it were, the various salients that Ludendorff had carved out represented very long frontages which required far more time, labour and building materials than were actually available. Thus relatively unsophisticated artillery preparations had been used against relatively unsophisticated fortifications.

The Flashing Sword of the Counter-Offensive

When it came to the Hindenburg Line, by contrast, everyone from Lloyd George downwards was acutely aware that the fortifications were very deep and well built, and had been in place ever since the winter of 1916–17. In this case it was felt that a long and careful preliminary bombardment would be absolutely essential. Some 1,600 guns opened fire on 26 September with a new type of mustard gas shell, switching to HE the next morning and following up during the next two days until the assault was finally unleashed at 5.50am on 29 September. Altogether some 750,000 shells were fired, although there were complaints that this was relatively light compared with some of the bombardments earlier in the war. Ammunition supply was especially difficult in the conditions of fast-moving warfare, which contrasted radically with the leisurely stockpiling that had been possible over weeks and months in the static warfare of previous years. The weather was also particularly bad in late September, which limited observation, particularly from the air. On the crucial sector between Bellicourt and Bony, where the American 27th and 30th Divisions were to attack across a 'land bridge' over the St Quentin Canal tunnel, there were further complications. Not all the approaches had been cleared of the enemy, but a number of small US detachments had become isolated behind enemy lines. This limited not only the observation that was available over the battlefield, but also the areas into which shells could be fired, for fear of hitting friendly troops. Altogether, therefore, the preliminary bombardment fell short of what would ideally have been required.

The main attack was to be by the Americans, supported by the Australians and some 165 tanks, over the Bellicourt 'land bridge'; yet this was the sector in which most difficulties and complications were encountered. A secondary attack by 46 (North Midland) Division was also planned further to the south, despite the protests of Monash, directly across the St Quentin Canal at a point opposite Bellenglise where it did not pass through a tunnel. This was widely considered to be a death trap, but the corps commander, General Walter Braithwaite, concocted an unlikely plan whereby the troops would use all sorts of ladders, ropes, light boats, life rafts and buoys to get across the canal by any possible means. He also arranged for sixteen tanks and a particularly large and impressive creeping barrage to precede the infantry on their attack frontage of 500 yards, and in the event this was totally successful. The Fourth Army was also lucky that its smoke shells on the morning of the attack were supplemented by a thick natural fog. The enemy was blinded, although the same was also true of the 337 allied aircraft that were available in support.

As the attack developed, it gradually became clear that although the two American divisions achieved as much as they possibly could, they had been asked to do too much. Their training and experience had not equipped them to follow a creeping barrage to the depth that was now expected, and in any case there were many problems with the way the barrage was laid on. A break-in was achieved on the Bellicourt 'land bridge', but it was frustratingly narrow and insufficiently deep. Too many German machine gunners remained active in the rear of the advancing spearheads, and the Australians had difficulty coming forward as the second echelon. Overall this attack, which it had been hoped would be decisive, fell below the expectations of the high command. On the other hand the unprepossessing 46th British Division achieved spectacularly more than expected. Suffering only light casualties, it swarmed down the hill through several enemy trench lines, and then straight across the fearsome canal itself. In some places it crossed a dry canal bed; at others it found light German bridges that had not been destroyed. Elsewhere its men had to swim or row, but all in all they got across and were ready to push onwards on the east bank by late morning. This constituted a remarkable feat of arms, and to this day it is still possible to find North Midland folk who take particular pride in the fact that it was their local boys – and not the much more famous Guards, Highlanders or ANZACs – who 'broke through the Hindenburg Line'.

In fact, however, there was a long way to go before the Hindenburg Line was fully broken, even though crossing the canal at Bellenglise had been an excellent start. A week of hard fighting still lay ahead, as the BEF's spearheads pressed forward through all the many preprepared rearward positions. The 'land bridge' over the canal tunnel was cleared at Bony only on 2 October, and the final defences of

The Flashing Sword of the Counter-Offensive

the Beaurevoir Line were securely in allied hands only by 6 October. The exceptional depth of the Siegfried position meant that it had to be ground down systematically over many days.

Nevertheless it was really just a matter of time, since it had now become obvious that the Germans were very seriously outclassed in almost every department. Quite apart from the vast quantities of territory, manpower and artillery that they had lost during the previous two months, the fighting morale of their soldiers remained questionable. They could show flashes of tactical resilience, and the tenacity of their rearguard machine gunners was legendary. Their staffwork and higher organization were still exemplary. However, the troops had been on short rations for many months, and they were acutely aware that their families at home in Germany were suffering even greater shortages. Since the failure of their 'peace offensive' of 15 July they had lost all faith in victory, and in their leaders. They had been pushed remorselessly back during the second half of 1916, and through most of 1917; now yet again they were being pushed back by an unprecedented series of allied attacks in the second half of 1918. By the start of October it was becoming increasingly clear to one and all that the German army was beaten.

On the allied side there were congenital optimists like Foch, who believed that nothing could go wrong as long as everyone attacked *à outrance*, and Haig, who had been confident for some time that it would all be over before Christmas. On the other hand there were pessimists like Pétain, who disagreed. In particular Haig's own chief of staff believed that the enemy was simply luring the BEF into a trap and would soon mount a fiendishly crushing counter-attack that would turn all the recent advances to dust. Such people would take some convincing. As for the Germans, Ludendorff apparently suffered a psychological fit on 28 September and on the following day advised the Kaiser that the war was lost. Both of them now realized that there was no longer any realistic hope that the war could last into 1919. Apart from anything else, their despised Austrian allies had also come to the end of their resolve and on 14 September had begun to make peace overtures. The allied forces in Salonika had finally advanced into the Balkans and were in the process of knocking

The Great War on the Western Front

Bulgaria out of the war. In Palestine General Allenby defeated the Turks at Megiddo on 19–21 September and was about to enter Damascus. Worst of all, however, was the rapidly deteriorating situation inside Germany itself.

After some bitter internal discussions and a change of government, on 4 October the Germans finally asked for an armistice and a peace settlement based on the US President Woodrow Wilson's 'Fourteen Points'. These amounted to an idealistic blueprint for peace on earth and happiness ever after which, although splendid as a statement of general principles, and alluring to the Central Powers, was lamentably short of either small print or an understanding of hard diplomatic realities. The Fourteen Points were deeply unacceptable to America's allies for a wide variety of reasons, and so both the negotiations and the war went on. The German armies continued their sullen retreat, and the allied armies continued to push forward as and when they managed to gather sufficient logistic and command resources for a new 'bite'. Overall their rate of advance averaged about one mile per day during three months, or a hundred miles in a hundred days. More significantly, perhaps, was the fact that in the last two or three weeks of this advance they were accelerating. The daily average in late October and early November was about twice what it had been in late August.

One notable incident came in the cavalry pursuit after the breaking of the Beaurevoir Line. On 9 October two cavalry brigades made a number of attacks on the road to Le Cateau which captured 500 prisoners, ten guns and no fewer than 150 machine guns. This action absolutely gives the lie to all the many sneering anti-cavalry commentaries that have constantly assured us that 'the machine gun made cavalry obsolete'. If it could capture 150 machine guns on a single day, then where is the problem? Which two brigades of infantry ever captured as many in such short order? Admittedly the cavalry did suffer some 600 casualties on that day, which was about the same as the Light Brigade at Balaklava, but on 9 October the British and Canadian cavalry opened the way to rather more of an operational advance than the Light Brigade ever did. Nor do we have to look far

114

The Flashing Sword of the Counter-Offensive

to find infantry brigades which lost many more than 600 casualties in a day on the Western Front.

After this, the Fourth Army found the enemy especially well dug in on the east bank of the river Selle, some twelve miles north-east of the Beaurevoir line. The second battle of Le Cateau did not begin until 17 October, and conditions were not good for either artillery observation or flying. The enemy fought back with unexpected tenacity, causing Haig an uncharacteristic moment of pessimism. Nevertheless by the 20th the British, including the two American divisions fighting with them, had pushed forward to the south of that town, and dislodged the Germans yet again. From there it was but four miles further to Ors, on the Sambre–Oise canal, and eight miles to Landrecies, just south of the looming forest of Mormal. All of these objectives were soon taken, and a canal-crossing operation was prepared on a wide front for 4 November. By this time British casualties were generally relatively light, although one of them was Captain Wilfred Owen, the poet, who fell on the canal bank north of Ors and was buried in the local village cemetery.

Meanwhile the First Army was approaching Valenciennes, which it had captured by 3 November, and the Third Army was closing on the ancient Vauban fortress of Le Quesnoy, which fell to the New Zealanders on the 4th. After this the road to Belgium was open, and during the period 5 to 11 November Haig's armies swept forward to take Maubeuge and finally Mons, the scene of the BEF's first battle of the war. To the north they had also taken Lille, Courtrai and Tournai, while the Belgians and French had cleared the coastline and were knocking on the gates of Ghent. To the south of the BEF the French had also advanced to the Belgian frontier and had almost reached Sedan.

This magnificent advance was not simply a factor of German weariness, starvation and moral collapse. It was also a technical triumph on the part of the allies, and perhaps more in the fields of logistics and staffwork than in those of tactics and heroics in the front line. We must remember that these armies had been formatted for the best part of four years as static organizations, advancing at best only a few hundred yards at a time, and relying on large stockpiles of supplies that had been laboriously pre-positioned over a period of weeks and months. During the 'Hundred Days', by contrast, they managed to make a rapid and successful transition to what at the time was called 'semi-mobile warfare', although in terms of miles advanced per day it was statistically no less mobile than the more celebrated allied advance from Normandy to the Baltic in 1944–5. To achieve this sustained offensive, much of the heavy equipment had to be left behind: for example, the supposedly 'war-winning' tanks could not be fielded in more than very small numbers except on 8 August and 29 September. More significantly for the style of fighting, the supply of artillery ammunition had to be slashed to a fraction of its normal scale as the fighting line advanced ever further ahead of its railheads and dumps. Equally the maintenance of communications became an ever growing headache, as telephone cable was consumed in unprecedented volumes and HQs moved from point to point in a disconcertingly rapid manner.

Overall since July the allies had captured over a third of a million Germans and 6,615 guns, although of course there were many more killed, wounded and missing Germans who did not become prisoners of war. The BEF had lost a third of a million overall casualties, which was still a high total. Up to the end this war continued to exact a heavy toll on its soldiers, even when they were making a war-winning offensive.

At 11.00am on 11 November an armistice finally came into force, some six weeks after Ludendorff's mental collapse of 28 September. Ludendorff himself had been dismissed from his command on 26 October, having left the 'home front' inside Germany in a state of near revolution. The High Seas Fleet had mutinied, demonstrations had spread to Berlin, and the army was in a state of obvious disarray. The Germans could no longer afford to continue the war, whereas the allies apparently could. When the German plenipotentiaries finally arrived in Foch's railway carriage at Compiègne on 8 November, they were forced to accept all the terms the allies demanded. Kaiser Wilhelm II abdicated on the following day and fled to Holland where he lived on, secure from legal retribution, until 1941.

The Flashing Sword of the Counter-Offensive

The Compiègne terms were the skeleton upon which the peace treaties of Versailles would be fleshed out in 1919–20, and in the long view of history we may say that they might have been drafted more wisely. In the short term, however, they brought the blissful, ever-longed-for, balm of true peace to the Western Front. The guns fell silent and the waiting battalions of monumental masons were at last let loose to do their work in every town and village of all the combatant nations. On the battlefields a carpet of ornamental cemeteries was rolled out to cradle the fallen, interspersed with some prestigious large constructions crafted by the most skilled architects in the world. The war had moved forward from its four years of lethality into a much longer era of sad remembrance.

CHAPTER NINE

The American Contribution to Victory

The American Contribution to Victory

Despite the post-war protestations of German soldiers that they were 'stabbed in the back' by shifty politicians and Bolshevik agitators at home, the fact is clear that the army itself had been comprehensively defeated on the battlefield. It had been kicked out of every defensive line it had attempted to hold; it had lost huge quantities of the essential war material it needed to continue the fight, especially artillery; and it had suffered a major degradation of its industrial base. The allied naval blockade had taken a long time to make a difference, but by 1918 it was biting deeply into the domestic economy upon which the army depended. The only sense in which the German army could claim to be 'undefeated' was the technical point that it was not chased all the way back onto German soil, so it did not suffer the humiliation of being defeated at home.

For the allied armies, by contrast, the key question was not so much 'did they win?', since obviously they did, but 'did they win against an effective enemy?' Those who accuse the allied generals of 1915–17 of being 'butchers and bunglers' would tell us that these same generals were successful in 1918 only because the enemy had to all intents and purposes collapsed. Therefore the military efficiency of the allied generals was no better than it ever had been: like Frederick the Great's legendary mule, they 'had participated in twenty campaigns but still learned nothing'.

On the other hand there are other commentators, including the present author, who believe that the allied generals did learn by experience, and had become better generals by the end of 1918 than they had been in earlier years. According to this critique the great allied assaults of the 'Hundred Days' would not have succeeded at all unless their commanders had achieved a marked improvement in technique. To take the most obvious example, Rawlinson's Fourth Army had made a most ghastly tactical mess of its attack on the Somme on 1 July 1916, but it charged triumphantly through all the German defences at Amiens on 8 August 1918. It was able to do this only because it had learned many new ways to use deception, artillery and tanks, which had not been understood or even imagined two years earlier. Beyond this, a whole additional set of techniques was required to keep the front line moving forward at the rate of one mile per day for all of three months. During 1915–17 the Western Front had been immobile, and all the practical lessons learned were based on static positional warfare. In 1918, by contrast, the fronts started to move much more fluidly, so a whole new art of war had to be invented. It cannot be stressed enough that the mere act of converting from static to mobile warfare represented a major technical innovation in its own right. It was not at all easy to arrange all the logistics, the signalling, the movement of artillery, the bridging, and a thousand other things that allowed the concept of 'mobility' to be translated from GHQ idealism into a realistic and practical method of daily operations. Unless the 'butchers and bunglers' had successfully risen to this particular challenge, they would have been doomed to leave the Germans, regardless of their particular level of combat efficiency, safely entrenched in their 'Winter Line', their Hindenburg Line, or their Selle Line south of Le Cateau. If this had happened, the war would surely have continued well into 1919.

Regardless of whether we condemn the allied generals as 'butchers and bunglers', we also have to confront yet another interpretation, which is that it was the American intervention that tipped the scales. Recent commentators such as John Mosier have even gone as far as to claim that the USA won the war.[1] However, this is a much more complex question than such writers have assumed, and to understand it correctly we have to go all the way back to the start of the war.

In 1914 the Americans, and their pacifist President Woodrow Wilson, were not at all anxious to become involved in what they saw as a typically degenerate European quarrel. The USA had been founded, among other things, as a safe haven for oppressed Europeans who wanted to escape from that sort of thing. In this new war her basic aim was to remain neutral while maintaining free trade with all the combatants, and freedom of navigation across all the oceans of the world. However, it soon became apparent that the allied navies were not going to allow quite those terms to apply. The conditions of their blockade meant that US ships could trade with other neutral countries or with the allies themselves, but not with Germany. This in

The American Contribution to Victory

turn meant that the American arms industries were forced to direct the fruits of their production towards the allies rather than the Central Powers, and in fact by the end of the war they had provided more powder and shell than all the native industries of Britain and France put together. To that extent it is profoundly true to say that the final victory on the Western Front could not have been achieved without the help of the USA.

This one-sided version of 'free trade' naturally incurred the wrath of the Germans, and in particular it attracted the attention of their submarines. As early as 7 May 1915 the proud British liner *Lusitania* was torpedoed and sunk while carrying munitions to Britain as well as passengers. Among the passengers 124 US citizens perished, and there was such a violent diplomatic storm that the Germans felt constrained to restrict the terms of engagement of their submarines for the next two years. Meanwhile Wilson attempted to put pressure on the western allies to make peace, although without success. Where he did succeed was in the presidential election of late 1916, when he was confirmed in office precisely because he had kept the USA out of the war. Paradoxically this stance did not survive for long, since Germany again declared unrestricted submarine warfare on 1 February 1917, and the intercepted 'Zimmermann Telegram' revealed that the Germans were plotting to support a Mexican attack on south-west USA, in clear contradiction of the Monroe Doctrine. Wilson and his government could no longer stand by as neutrals, especially since by this time the Western allies were so deeply in debt to the Americans that Wall Street could not possibly contemplate an allied defeat. In financial terms the USA was forced to throw her weight behind an allied victory, on pain of losing the value of her already vast investment in allied munitions and loans.

The Americans entered the war on the allied side on 6 April 1917, with an army that was absolutely tiny by European standards. It would take a very long time to build it up to a respectable size, and even longer to ship it to France. At that point it was obvious why the Germans had calculated that the benefits of stopping the huge flow of munitions to Europe by U-boat warfare greatly outweighed the risk of finding at best 100,000 US troops deployed on the Western Front in 1917 or early 1918.

As we have seen in previous chapters, there were some US troops already in action against the German spring offensives of 1918: at Villers-Bretonneux, Cantigny and then on the Marne, most notably at Château Thierry and Belleau Wood. However these actions, all most useful to the allied cause, were relatively small in scale, normally involving just a couple of divisions, although four US divisions would go into action together at the end of June in the Soissons counter-attack. But it was only around St Mihiel on 12 September 1918 that as many as seven divisions could be deployed together, that is, some nineteen months after the original declaration of unrestricted submarine warfare. The Germans were therefore quite right to believe that they would have all of that time to win the war in the west, and in the event they very nearly succeeded.

Apart from their massive shipments of powder and shell, the American contribution to victory consisted partly of the troops that they did deploy to France before the armistice, of which some 1,390,000 eventually saw active service at the front, and partly of the additional million that were still on the way, threatening to have as many as 3,000,000 troops available to join the battle in 1919. From the German point of view the US troops who were in action during 1918 were irksome and damaging enough, but the far more numerous troops who might have entered the fight in the following year would have been absolutely decisive. This was also the view of General Pershing, who was always insistent on keeping his American troops together in one army which could eventually win the war on its own. Indeed, he sometimes seemed to think that he could still win the war even if all his other allies had totally collapsed.

Besides the constant pleas from his allies to release troops piecemeal into the fighting line, Pershing's main problem was shipping. There were only so many ships available to bring American and Canadian men and munitions to Europe, not to mention food supplies to supplement the diet of the British people under U-boat blockade. By the end of March 1918 there were sufficient troops available in the USA for an accelerated programme of shipping to

The American Contribution to Victory

be arranged; 120,000 men were to make the voyage every month for four months, making almost half a million by the end of July. However these men were to be just the fighting elements of each division, excluding their supporting and logistic organizations, as well as anything by way of heavy weapons. Very few aircraft or artillery pieces would make the journey from the USA to France, and no tanks. This meant that the AEF would take on a very odd structure: short on logistics and other support troops, but exceptionally heavy on front-line infantry. In fact an American infantry division was almost 28,000 strong, at a time when allied divisions were usually something like 12,000 and those of the Germans smaller still. The American troops were also almost totally supplied by Britain and France. All their tanks and tin hats, and most of their aircraft, machine guns, artillery and transport were provided from European sources.

There was also a problem with training. The American troops were physically very fit and often impressively tall by comparison with their European comrades. They brought with them a breath of fresh air, because they had not experienced the grinding hecatombs of Verdun, the Somme, the Chemin des Dames or Passchendaele. Yet this 'lack of experience' could be seen as another name for naivety. On many occasions detachments of US troops were sent on training courses with the British or French armies, only to disappoint their teachers by their refusal to learn. 'Don't worry, we'll do it in our own way' was an often-heard mantra that invariably infuriated their allies who had seen modern battle at close range. The Europeans knew only too well what would happen, but they found themselves frustratingly powerless to impart this knowledge to their over-confident students.

When they were on the defensive at Villers-Bretonneux, Château Thierry and elsewhere, American troops performed very well. In the attack, by contrast, they displayed much less certainty of touch. At Belleau Wood, for example, the marines made very heavy weather of their assaults. Admittedly the light resistance offered to the US advance into the St Mihiel salient may possibly have created an excessive confidence in the American art of attack, but if so, disillusionment would not be long delayed in the Argonne.

THE MEUSE-ARGONNE

The battle of the Meuse-Argonne, which started on 26 September and lasted for all the rest of the war, would cost 117,000 US casualties as well as a large number of French (which seems to be as unspecified in US sources as the French losses on the Somme are unspecified in British sources). Initially some fifteen US and twenty-seven French infantry divisions were committed, as well as four French cavalry divisions, although the large size of the American divisions made them the equivalent of some thirty French infantry divisions. The dividing line between the French and the Americans was the western edge of the Argonne forest, which meant that the US troops had the unenviable task of clearing this dense and heavily defended terrain, although admittedly they had the benefit of some clearer and more open ground to the east of the forest.

The first day of the battle went reasonably well, but problems soon arose thereafter. In particular the American logistics collapsed and there were fantastic traffic jams, on a scale that no one had ever seen before. There were reports of officers attempting to get the traffic moving by discharging their revolvers but, unsurprisingly, this technique did not appear to work. Many symptoms were encountered of the same type of tactical naivety that the British had displayed on the Somme and the French in 1915. Not only were there many instances of sacrificial frontal attacks which had not been properly prepared, but reported 'gas casualties' were running at about ten times the level known on any other battlefield. This entitles us to suspect that most cases were just bad smells that were misinterpreted by inexperienced troops, rather than actual poison gas. By 5 October the US offensive had ground to a halt in the enemy's second defensive line, until a new impetus and reorganization could be imposed.

By the time the war ended, the battle had been pushed forward in two major new impulses: one on 14 October that made little pro-

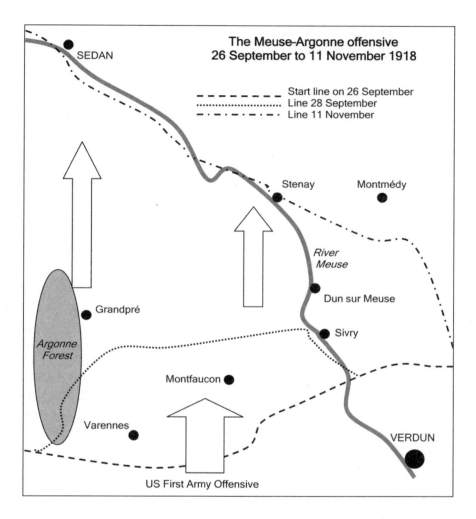

The Meuse-Argonne offensive
26 September to 11 November 1918

- - - - - - Start line on 26 September
.... Line 28 September
- · - · - · - Line 11 November

SEDAN

Stenay Montmédy

River
Meuse

Dun sur Meuse

Grandpré

Sivry

Argonne
Forest

Montfaucon

Varennes

VERDUN

US First Army Offensive

gress, and another on 1 November that made much better headway. Sedan was liberated to the French on 6 November, and it can be said that by that date the US armies had learned many things about modern warfare that they had not suspected in September. Nobody thought he understood this better than Pershing himself, and just before the armistice he raged that his single-handed American victory had been dashed from his hands by the cessation of hostilities: 'If they had given us another ten days, we would have rounded up the entire German army, captured it, humiliated it ... Had they given us another week, we'd have taught them.'[2] This perspective was excessive in the extreme and it is notable that the BEF, who had surely pushed forward harder and faster in the last three months of the war, did not display any comparable euphoria. Haig and his generals knew exactly how big and formidable the German army still remained, even if 'Black Jack' Pershing apparently did not.

What Pershing really meant, we must suppose, was that if the war had continued into 1919, then the Americans might well have been in a position to take the lead in an advance into Germany. He may have been right, except that the city of Metz was the first target he had in mind, just as it had already been before the St Mihiel offensive in early September. Pershing seemed to be mesmerized by the thought that Metz was very close to the area of operations of the AEF and was also technically inside Germany. It was a major city in the part of Lorraine that had been occupied in 1871, and as such it formed a significant element in the *casus belli* of 1914. It would have made a famous symbolic victory if he had captured it. However, what Pershing overlooked was the fact that ever since 1871 Metz had been fortified by the Germans to at least the same standard that the French had applied to Verdun during the same period. To attack Metz in 1919 would have been equivalent to selecting the very strongest point in the enemy line upon which to beat one's head. Success would not by any means have been guaranteed, as General George Patton would discover in late 1944, when he in turn attempted to capture the Metz defences with a quick attack, only to find himself bogged down in a fruitless struggle that lasted several months.

Beyond Pershing's personal frustration that the Meuse-Argonne battle was terminated by the armistice just as the AEF was finally getting into its stride, there was another and deeper frustration that would mark the US armed forces for much of the twentieth century. This may be simply expressed as a frustration that the Americans were never really allowed to demonstrate what they could do. They had been participating in this war on a large scale for just two months before it ended. They had lost 'only' about 52,000 dead and 255,896 total casualties, almost half of them in the Meuse-Argonne. This was fewer even than the Canadians' 59,000 killed in the whole war, out of 208,700 total casualties, whereas the French had been fighting for four years and had lost 1,385,300 dead, and the UK had lost 702,410.[3] Also in the Meuse-Argonne, the major American effort of the war, their troops had not obviously distinguished themselves. They had become entangled in the traffic jams, in the forest, in the wire, in the supposed 'gas clouds', and in the notoriously interlocking fields of fire of the German machine guns. All in all, it was not a glorious performance, and this would have two main consequences.

In the first place the Meuse-Argonne experience meant that the First World War as a whole somewhat slipped out of the American military consciousness. It had been a major national effort, but it had ended as something of a damp squib. People like Pershing might have blustered that the whole German army lay at their mercy, but the ordinary American soldier saw only a futile exercise in hardship, deprivation and danger. Nor did the hardships stop when the war ended and the army was demobilized, since many of the troops found it hard to find a job in the bleak civilian landscape of the 1920s. US historians have subsequently tended to dismiss the whole sequence of mobilization, combat and demobilization as 'futile', without enquiring very much further, and have echoed the Wilsonian critique of 1914–16 that the war was never really any of America's business anyway. Perhaps it would be best to forget all about it. The US political classes made an even swifter decision in the same direction, by voting Wilson out of office in 1920, while refusing to ratify his beloved plans for the League of Nations.

Secondly, the Meuse-Argonne battle seems to have imprinted the myth of the 'ten-foot-high German' into the American military consciousness. In Britain the experience of being shot down in thousands on 1 July 1916 seems to have created a belief that their own generals were butchers and bunglers. In the USA, by contrast, the experience of being shot down in October 1918 seems to have created a belief that the Germans facing them were remarkably fine soldiers and the epitome of all military virtues. During the remainder

of the twentieth century this idea, which would be reinforced in many
hard battles during the Second World War, bored its way into so
much of American military literature that by the 1980s it had become
axiomatic that anything the Germans ever did was fantastically
wonderful, while anything done by any other nation's army was
distinctly mediocre. So far did this bizarre cult go that the US Army
even adopted a version of the German pot helmet for its infantry,
although no one apparently stopped to ask if the Germans had
actually won either of their two world wars. To the present author it
seems that this whole movement can be traced back, precisely, to the
Meuse-Argonne battle. Before that, apart from the influence of the
German von Steuben during the revolutionary war, it had always
been France that had filled the role of 'the USA's most admired
military nation'. It was certainly apparent during the Great War that
the Americans' commanders, if not perhaps their men, preferred to
fight alongside their French rather than their British allies.

However that may be, there was also a third, and arguably no less
important set of lessons that the US Army took away from the
Meuse-Argonne offensive. These consisted of the much more personal and specific experiences of its officers who would later rise to
occupy eminent positions during the Second World War and thereafter, most notably George C Marshall, Douglas MacArthur and
George Patton. These men would come away from the war with very
different perspectives upon it, since they had each held very different
posts within the army's chain of command. Marshall had been a key
figure on Pershing's planning staff throughout hostilities, whereas
MacArthur, despite Pershing's specific disapproval, had started as
chief of staff to the National Guard 'Rainbow Division' (the third US
division to arrive in France), and thereafter won fame as a pugnacious
and effective brigade commander in the front line. Patton was different again, since his career had begun in Pershing's beloved cavalry,
but he had then progressed into tanks, which Pershing distrusted
deeply. He became a leading pioneer of armour but, along with the
future president Dwight D Eisenhower (who did not serve in France
but conducted tank training near Gettysburg in 1918), he soon
discovered that enthusiasm for tanks was not a career-enhancing

The American Contribution to Victory

characteristic in the post-war army. Two other Second World War leaders should also be mentioned here. In common with MacArthur, lieutenants Mark Clark and Omar Bradley both fought in the front line, and both were critical of the tactics being employed. Thus the lessons they took away from the Meuse-Argonne were of the 'how not to do it' kind.

CHAPTER TEN

The Western Front as a Historiographical Phenomenon

The Western Front as a Historiographical Phenomenon

Quite apart from the special case of the Americans, the Western Front rapidly became a focus of fierce controversy in both France and Britain. During the war itself there had been some public criticisms of the way the war was being run, most notably by conscientious objectors and pacifist groups, not to mention the French mutineers, even though the latter's critique was maintained as a military secret with considerable success. In Britain Captain Siegfried Sassoon made a public denunciation of the war in the summer of 1917, and was sent to a psychiatric hospital for his pains.[1] Politicians were sometimes forced to resign over particular policies, as was Churchill over the Dardanelles, although more often their strenuous debates were kept behind closed doors. In every country it was much more common for generals to be sacked for real or imagined mistakes, most spectacularly Nivelle and Gough, and a colourful vocabulary emerged to describe the process. In the Boer War the victims had been sent to the depot at Stellenbosch, hence they were 'Stellenbosched'. Under Joffre the French miscreants were sent to Limoges, hence 'Limogé', or they were simply 'dégommé', which in English means 'unstuck' but which was more often translated directly as 'de-gummed'. Even then, however, their dismissal could be construed less as a criticism of the war than as a resolution by the higher authorities to pursue it ever more efficiently in future.

Most public pronouncements reported in the press were supportive of the war, or at least not openly critical. A considerable effort went into censorship, and indeed into active propaganda for the benefit of both friendly and enemy populations. Nevertheless the censors could not conceal the fact that particular battles had bogged down when breakthroughs had been hoped for, nor that casualties were always running at an exceptionally high level. Soldiers' letters home could be censored, but their conversations when they were home on leave could not. Private photography at the front was banned, but the official photographers who were given access could scarcely conceal the fact that the battlefields had been reduced to a mud-scape in which all the trees and buildings had been levelled and the soldiers lived in slimy holes in the ground. The horrors of trench warfare could not really be kept secret at the time, although it was never translated into widespread civilian protests. Much more common was industrial action against poor working conditions in the factories, or grumbling against food shortages or air raids. Everyone obviously longed for peace, but for most people outside Russia – and Germany during the last month – the way to achieve it seemed to be through victory rather than subversion.

This consensus held together during the early days after the armistice, but it was gradually eroded from a number of different directions. In the first place the true and shocking scale of the casualties became an unavoidable public fact as vast numbers of monuments and military cemeteries were built. Admittedly the Germans were not allowed to build any such cemeteries on French soil until 1924, by which time the mortal remains of large numbers of their fallen had become entirely irretrievable. Therefore the scale of their burials was very much smaller than that of the allies, which tended to reinforce the general impression that the Germans, with their inconspicuous grey crosses, had suffered far fewer casualties than the British and French, who displayed unmissable fields of brilliant white crosses and Portland stone gravestones.

Meanwhile the Imperial War Museum in London, the Australian War Memorial in Canberra and a variety of French peepshows and memorial museums were also presenting photographs, paintings and archives to the public that vividly illustrated the squalid but previously hidden conditions of modern battle. Parades and other ceremonies were held on a regular basis to commemorate the fallen. At first they centred on 1–2 November, which had long been observed as a time of remembrance.[2] However, they later crystallized around 11 November, the actual date of the armistice. Earl Haig's own post-war role was as head of the British Legion, which was set up to support veterans, and his annual poppy appeal has made a particularly visible display of popular solidarity with the cause of remembrance right up to the present day.

Secondly, the trench poetry and soldiers' memoirs began to be published, presenting the public with the raw personal emotions that

The Western Front as a Historiographical Phenomenon

had previously been suppressed in the formal official reporting, and detonating a widespread surge of pacifism and anti-militarism. At first this was just a trickle, but when Robert Graves published his *Goodbye to All That* in 1929,[3] it quickly became a flood. The year 1930 was a bumper one for publishing this type of literature, although it is perhaps remarkable that so little of it had surfaced earlier. Indeed, some of it is still appearing for the first time only in the modern age. For example, one item that was published locally in Scotland in 1930 was a play entitled *The Prayer*, written by a former stretcher-bearer, William St Clair. This reached a national audience, together with almost 200 pages of depressed and angry letters from the front, only in 2004.[4] This volume is no less biting than many of the more famous earlier publications, and if it had entered the national consciousness in 1930 it would surely have had just the same impact that they did.

Alongside the personal testimonies of the men at the bottom of the tree, there was a third strand in the critique, which was arguably the most influential of all. This was the 'top down' view from politicians who, like Clemenceau, believed that 'war is far too important to be left to generals'. Taking the lead in this movement were the wartime prime minister, David Lloyd George, and Winston Churchill, who would be the prime minister in the next war. As we have already seen, both of them had deep political reasons for finding an alternative to the 'Western Front' strategy favoured by the leading generals, and thereby refusing to accept the obvious truth that if France had fallen, total German hegemony in Europe was all but assured. As politicians they needed to assert their supremacy over the army, and this often meant denigrating the generals. Their war memoirs, when they appeared in 1934–6 and 1923–31 respectively, constituted a frontal assault on the military reputations of many high commanders, most notably Haig himself, especially over the sensitive matter of Passchendaele.

In this endeavour they were supported by a number of supposedly 'reputable' journalists and other respected figures who were even quicker to point the finger of blame. There was, for example, a school of tacticians who had their own names to make. When General Sir

The Great War on the Western Front

Ivor Maxse was de-gummed for his central role in the defeat of 21 March 1918, he was then appointed to take charge of writing tactical manuals. It served his ambition to deny that any of the 300-odd BEF manuals that had already been written possessed any merit at all, although his own infantry manual then appeared somewhat unhelpfully only after the war had ended. What Maxse was saying, in effect, was that all the authors of previous manuals had been incompetent, which was both extraordinarily unfair and factually wrong. Then as early as 1921 a new self-regarding star appeared in this area, in the shape of Captain (retired) Basil 'Liddell' Hart. He went one step further and asserted that there had been no tactics at all during the war – presumably not even Maxse's. It was only he, Hart, who was inventing the tactics for the twentieth century, even though a specialist might note that the manual that he actually produced was almost word-for-word the same as the one that had already been issued to British troops in February 1917. This, however, was only an opening salvo, since Hart went on to fill the newspapers with all sorts of claims that the war should have been fought in the eastern theatres, rather than France; that 'indirect approaches' should have been found; and that it would probably have been better not to use an army at all, but to win the whole thing by strategic bombing. Hart was extraordinarily influential during the inter-war period, basically for alleging that the high command had been incompetent in 1914–18, and trading on the general hope that 'there would be no more Passchendaeles'.

Hart's friend J F C Fuller was another notorious maverick who had a habit of grabbing attention through the newspapers. He had been a leading staff officer for the tank corps during the war, and hence a writer of some of the manuals that Maxse and Hart affected to despise, but as a disciple of the devil-worshipper Aleister Crowley it must be said that he harboured a very odd view of the world indeed. His main disservice to the inter-war debate was to propagate the entirely erroneous idea that Haig and other ex-cavalry generals had been prejudiced against the tank corps and had tried to close it down. This was pure paranoia, which was unfortunately prolonged through the 1930s when tanks really did become a low budgetary priority,

The Western Front as a Historiographical Phenomenon

albeit only for the single and simple reason that the army as a whole was a low budgetary priority – by contrast, for example, with Hart's beloved strategic bombers. By that time, however, Fuller had left the army and had become a fascist, so his direct influence waned. But the damage had already been done.

One of the most directly critical books that appeared before the explosion of the 'poets and novelists' movement in 1929–30 had been *Lions Led by Donkeys*, written by P A Thompson in 1927. This was an analysis of British generalship, mostly limited to 1914–15, which unsparingly highlighted all the defects of that particularly chaotic period. The author did not care to examine the later achievements of BEF generalship during the period when there were sixty divisions in line rather than merely a dozen; but his main literary success was that the title he had chosen became indelibly etched onto any discussion of the Western Front forever afterwards. Apparently it had already been a well-known French phrase from 1870, but now Thompson gave it a second career as a cliché in the Anglo-Saxon world with reference to the BEF.

While we are considering the inter-war literature, we must certainly mention the so-called 'Official Histories', which would eventually run to several score of volumes of text, maps and orders of battle. In France they were written in an impersonal and formal style, by a committee. In Britain, however, the general editor, Brigadier James Edmonds, brought a much more personal, not to say prejudiced, approach. The author of each volume was a named individual who was allowed a certain degree of initiative. Much of what they wrote was a dry technical narrative, but occasionally a flash of 'office politics' shows through. Edmonds himself, for example, sometimes allows himself to be very rude about the French, in a way that would surely not have been officially approved if it had been brought to the attention of the Foreign Office.

One particularly noteworthy official historian was G C Wynne, who wrote the volumes about the BEF in 1915. Studying the bleak results of these botched battles apparently drove him into a personal depression from which he emerged not only as a believer in the 'lions led by donkeys' theory, but also as a great admirer of the German art of war. In the 1930s he wrote some influential studies in praise of their depth defence tactics, thereby helping to propagate the myth of the ten-foot-high German. Another influential critic of British generalship was C E W Bean, the official historian of the Australian contribution to victory. With all the brashness and assertiveness to be expected from that fledgling nation, he lost no opportunity to slate the Pommy leadership and to explain how it was always the Australians who saved the day, and ultimately won the war. This brand of mythology struck a deep chord in antipodean hearts, and it is still widely believed today.

THE SECOND GENERATION

The 1930s were marked by a growth in Western fears that if the first great war had been terrible, the next one would be terminal. Idealistic hopes that the League of Nations would make future wars impossible had evaporated the moment the USA refused to join it, whereas the rise of militaristic dictatorships in the USSR, Italy, Japan, Spain and especially Germany made it very difficult indeed to believe that international peace would last for very long. Everyone was also aware that the Great War had spawned many novel instruments of frightfulness, from poison gas, unrestricted U-boat warfare and strategic bombing, all the way down to flame throwers, hand grenades and even sub-machine guns. Oddly, artillery, which was the main purveyor of death, was not widely identified in the public mind as anything particularly new. Artillery had of course existed since at least the fifteenth century, and (to the uninformed) not even 'the HE revolution' and other crucial upgrades between 1880 and 1900 had seemed to break very far from the past. What the general public did not seem to understand was that if there had been an 'artillery revolution' in the late Victorian era, there had been no less than a 'mega-revolution' between 1916 and 1918.

What did seize the imagination of the general public was the hidden menace of *future* perverted science. During the war everyone had observed the extent to which states were secretly mobilizing their brainpower and industries to create deadly new weapons, and there

The Western Front as a Historiographical Phenomenon

seemed to be no particularly good reason why they should break off from doing so in 1919. One does not have to look far to find projections into the future whereby cities the size of London or Berlin could be totally destroyed by a fiendish combination of HE, gas and incendiary bombs within the space of a few days. Admittedly this type of result would not in fact be technically possible until 1945, when it was demonstrated at Dresden, Tokyo, Hiroshima and Nagasaki, but it was far from unrealistic for the press to express fears about such things a decade earlier. On the contrary, since few in the 1930s had seriously envisaged a major industrial power attempting to commit genocide on the scale that Nazi Germany actually did in the 1940s, we can even perhaps accuse the general public of a certain lack of fearful imagination, rather than an excess of it.

The Second World War began with professional soldiers, no less than pacifists, resolved that there should be 'No more Passchendaeles' or, in German, 'Nie wieder Verdun'. Each army envisaged a different way of achieving this objective. In France Maginot's solution was to build a super-Verdun fortress all along the frontier that would not be as vulnerable to an initial attack as the prototype had been in February 1916. In Germany the idea was for short, sharp 'lightning wars' that would cut through the enemy defences with mechanized spearheads, thereby avoiding prolonged battles of attrition. In Britain, however, the solution was much less universally agreed, presumably because the army was a Cinderella service when compared with the navy and RAF, and there was no clarity about either national strategy or military doctrine. It nevertheless remained true that on a number of occasions senior officers shied away from mounting offensives for fear of sinking into a battle of attrition. Even in Germany there were grave professional doubts about attacking the strong defences of the Czech Sudetenland as well as the Maginot system, and then about the bold movement through the Ardennes into France in 1940 on an alarmingly narrow front.

Despite these early misgivings, the world's armies soon found themselves reverting to trench warfare that was every bit as costly as anything seen at Passchendaele or Verdun. In Stalingrad, Normandy and even as far afield as Iwo Jima and Okinawa the bad old processes

The Great War on the Western Front

of *Zermerbungskrieg* came back into play in a way that von Falken-hayn would surely have approved. More specifically still, in the Korean War the UN forces would mount the appropriately named 'Operation Killer', which was designed to grind down the Chinese army by pure attrition. The spirit of Verdun lived on.

The Second World War eventually cost more than six times as many casualties as the Western Front, although its result seemed somehow less futile and more decisive. For example, the democratic Germany that emerged from it was far stronger and has lasted far longer than the Weimar Republic that came out of the Treaty of Versailles in 1919. The public nevertheless remained dimly aware that war itself was a bad thing, so they were still prepared to return to the Western Front as a 'classic' and well-documented illustration of its horrors. In the 1960s there was a new wave of pacifism as National Service was abolished in Britain and global anti-war senti-ment was provoked by American operations in Vietnam. In this climate the debate about the Western Front was reborn. Books such as Corelli Barnett's *The Swordbearers*, on various high commanders, and Alistair Horne's *The Price of Glory* on Verdun, made a great impact. Even more telling was Joan Littlewood's theatrical produc-tion of *Oh What a Lovely War*,[5] which appeared in 1963, to be followed by an influential film in 1969. This constituted a ferocious frontal attack on the generals of the Western Front as donkeys, butchers, bunglers and whatever other insults one might like to invent. On the other hand the epic 1965 BBC TV series *The Great War* by Tony Essex, with historical advice mainly by John Terraine, was much better researched and historically balanced. However, its main impact was through contemporary photographs and films, and many of these were unavoidably horrific. Without being particularly intended, the message propagated by the medium acted as a re-inforcement of Joan Littlewood's propaganda. A solid consensus formed that the Western Front was uniquely horrible and its generals were uniquely incompetent. John Terraine himself wrote a series of books protesting at this interpretation, but he was very much a lone voice and he was cruelly mocked in fashionable circles by people who

The Western Front as a Historiographical Phenomenon

knew much less about historical realities than about whichever vacuous opinions happened to be in vogue.

Since the 1980s a new breed of military historians has increasingly applied rigorous research techniques to the story of the Western Front, treating it no longer as some sort of sacred literary parable for doomed youth, but rather as a war that had to be fought according to military logic, just like any other war. Many books have appeared in this vein, not least by the Australian scholars Robin Prior and Trevor Wilson who, although perhaps still of the 'lions led by donkeys' persuasion, have nevertheless taken the trouble to analyze the archives carefully rather than uncritically printing the legend. British students at the Imperial War Museum, King's College London, and more recently the University of Birmingham, have studied the same archives in more of a 'lions led by lions' frame of mind, to revealing effect. The impressive continuing activities of the Western Front Association have also helped to propagate their message more widely. This has not, alas, prevented the fashionable literary, television and cinematographic élite from churning out ever more of the sad old propaganda, and selling at least ten books to every one sold by scholarly military historians. The general public remains convinced that the war to save Europe from an aggressive German hegemony was totally futile, even though the second war to achieve the same objective meets general approval. It is also widely believed that the men who fought on the Western Front to liberate Belgium and France were fools who blindly accepted the orders issued by butchers and bunglers which sent them to their deaths. The fact that both the soldiers and their generals actually won the war, and were mostly proud of their achievement, appears to have been lost somewhere along the way.

Notes

Chapter 1. The Start of the War and of the Western Front

1. For a collection of modern discussions see Richard F Hamilton and Holger H Herwig (eds), *The Origins of World War I* (Cambridge: Cambridge University Press, 2003). The classic account is Luigi Albertini, *The Origins of the War of 1914*, trans. Isabella Massey, 3 vols (Oxford: Oxford University Press, 1952).
2. The status of this as a firm 'plan' has recently been questioned by Terence Zuber, *Inventing the Schlieffen Plan: German War Planning 1871–1914* (Oxford: Oxford University Press, 2002).
3. See the works of Gustave Le Bon; see especially R A Nye, *The Origins of Crowd Psychology* (London: SAGE, 1975), chapter 6. See also discussion in Paddy Griffith, *Forward into Battle*, (2nd edn, Swindon: Crowood Press, 1990), pp. 84–94.

Chapter 2. Late 1914 and the Battles of 1915: Birth of a New Style of Warfare

1. See commentary in J P Harris, *Men, Ideas and Tanks: British Military Thought and Armoured Forces, 1903–39* (Manchester: Manchester University Press, 1995), pp. 4–8.
2. Tony Ashworth, *Trench Warfare 1914–18: the Live and Let Live System* (London: Macmillan, 1980).
3. Ibid., pp. 24–8 and *passim*.
4. 1/4th battalion of the Berkshire regiment: ibid., p. 15.
5. *Some Principles of Maritime Strategy* (first published 1911; new edn, London: Brassey's, 1988).

The Great War on the Western Front

Chapter 3.   The Battle of Verdun, 1916

1. Bruce Gudmundsson, *Stormtroop Tactics: Innovation in the German Army, 1914–18* (New York: Praeger, 1989).
2. Alistair Horne, *The Price of Glory* (London: Macmillan, 1962), p. 327; but Anthony Bruce, *An Illustrated Companion to the First World War* (London: Michael Joseph, 1989) puts the total casualties at 950,000 for both sides.

Chapter 4.   The Battle of the Somme, 1916

1. These statistics have not stopped many commentators wrongly asserting that there were '60,000 dead'.
2. Harris, *Men, Ideas and Tanks*, p. 67.
3. The exact numbers are still disputed to this day, although the work of Sir Charles Oman retains its value: 'The German losses on the Somme', in Lord Sydenham of Combe (ed.), *'The World Crisis' by Winston Churchill: a Criticism* (London, 1927).
4. See especially Christopher Duffy, *Through German Eyes: the British and the Somme, 1916* (London: Weidenfeld, 2006).
5. *The Storm of Steel* (first English edn 1929; new edn, London: Constable, 1994), p. 107.
6. Ibid., p. 109.
7. Ibid., p. 110.
8. A recent English-language study of French army morale is Leonard V Smith, *Between Mutiny and Obedience: the Case of the French Fifth Infantry Division during World War I* (New Jersey: Princeton University Press, 1994).
9. English Mayflower edn, London, 1963.
10. *Under Fire: the Story of a Squad* (first published as *Le Feu*, 1917; English Everyman edn, London, 1926).
11. The first two lines of 'Anthem for Doomed Youth', in Brian Gardner (ed.), *Up the Line to Death: the War Poets 1914–18* (first published 1964; Magnum edn, London, 1977), p. 136.
12. A striking analysis of the pre-war literary basis of the trench writings is Paul Fussell, *The Great War and Modern Memory* (Oxford: Oxford University Press, 1975).

Notes

13. Julian Putkowski and Julian Sykes, *Shot at Dawn: Executions in World War One by Authority of the British Army Act* (London: Leo Cooper, 1989). See also Julian Putkowski, *British Army Mutineers 1914–1922* (London: Francis Boutle, 1998).

Chapter 7.   The Bitter Winter of 1917–18

1. It was perhaps no coincidence that the Royal Air Force was founded at just this time, by the amalgamation of the Royal Flying Corps with the Royal Naval Air Service.
2. See James Sambrook, *With the Rank and Pay of a Sapper: the 216th [Nuneaton] Army Troops Company, Royal Engineers, in the Great War* (Nuneaton: Paddy Griffith Associates, 1998). An engaging account of some of the men who helped stop Ludendorff's March 1918 offensive outside Villers-Bretonneux, and went on to provide the essential bridging for Fourth Army's advances in the 'Hundred Days'.
3. Joffre had been promoted into the marshalate, but out of his command, in December 1916. Pétain would be made a marshal at the end of 1918.

Chapter 8.   The Flashing Sword of the Counter-Offensive

1. Britain procured a total of some 55,000 aircraft in the war, or an average of 1,100 per month. Of these, she lost some 36,000 to all causes (65 per cent), including 4,000 in combat (7 per cent). The figures for Germany were slightly less and those for France rather more: see my *Battle Tactics of the Western Front: the British Army's Art of Attack, 1916–18* (New Haven and London: Yale University Press, 1994), p. 252; Michael Cox and John Ellis, *The World War I Databook* (London: Aurum Press, 1993), pp. 254–61, 281.

Chapter 9.   The American Contribution to Victory

1. *The Myth of the Great War: A New Military History of World War One. How the Germans Won the Battles and How the Americans Saved the Allies* (London: Profile Books, 2001).

2. Paul F Braim, *The Test of Battle: the American Expeditionary Forces in the Meuse-Argonne Campaign* (first published 1987; new edn, Shippensburg, PA: White Mane Books, 1998), p. 139, quoting Donald Smythe.
3. Cox and Ellis, *The World War I Databook*, pp. 269–70.

Chapter 10.   The Western Front as a Historiographical Phenomenon

1. Siegfried Sassoon, *Memoirs of an Infantry Officer* (first edn 1930; new edn, London: Faber & Faber, 1965).
2. i.e. All Saints' or All Hallows' Day, followed by All Souls' Day. In Latin America this season is associated with 'the day of the dead'.
3. London: Jonathan Cape.
4. William St Clair, *The Road to St Julien: the Letters of a Stretcher-Bearer from the Great War*, ed. John St Clair (Barnsley: Leo Cooper, 2004).
5. Joan Littlewood (ed.), *Oh What a Lovely War* (first published 1965; new edn, London: Methuen Drama, 2000).

Glossary of Terms

AEF – American Expeditionary Force.

ANZAC – Originally the Australian and New Zealand Army Corps, although the contingents from the two countries were later separated, with the more numerous Australians eventually settling as a corps of five divisions, which enjoyed a unique reputation for self-regard and Pommy-bashing as much as for its high skills of aggressive patrolling and combat efficiency.

BEF – British Expeditionary Force to France and Belgium.

Casualties – This term includes dead, wounded, missing and prisoners. It must *not* be confused, as it too often is, with the total of dead (which in this war usually ran at something like a third of the total casualties).

chevaux de frise – A row of metal or timber spikes held together on a timber frame, used as a military obstacle for several centuries before barbed wire was invented, but anachronistically still in use during the Great War.

GHQ – General Headquarters of the BEF, i.e. the command staff of first French and then Haig.

HE – High Explosive.

Kitchener or **'New' Armies** – The mass mobilization of 'hostilities only' volunteers in 1914–15 which produced a majority of the BEF of 1916, largely replacing the regulars and territorials who had started the war. In late 1916 the supply of volunteers had dried up, so conscription was at last introduced in Britain.

der Millionenkrieg – War fought by millions of men, which was one of the most striking innovations of 1914–18. Some armies had

149

technically fielded over a million men at a time in years before 1914, but only in the Great War would such large numbers be present on the same front.

No man's land – The 'neutral' ground between two opposing lines of trenches. It was a notoriously dangerous place to be, since it was potentially under fire from both sides, but on many nights it was surprisingly heavily populated by wiring parties and offensive or defensive patrols.

Pom (noun), **Pommy** (adj.) – Derogatory Australian term for a Briton.

Schwerpunkt – The key point on the battlefield. German doctrine recommended that an absolute maximum of resources should be concentrated there, even if that left other important points under-provided.

Further Reading: A Short Annotated Bibliography

Technical and Narrative Studies

Tony Ashworth, *Trench Warfare 1914–18: the Live and Let Live System* (London: Macmillan, 1980). Splendid analysis of how the war wasn't fought on the 'quiet' sections of the front.

Correlli Barnett, *The Swordbearers: Studies in Supreme Command in the First World War* (first published London: Eyre & Spottiswoode, 1963). Excellent studies of some of the key commanders of all nations, in some of the key battles.

John Bourne and Gary Sheffield (eds), *The War Diaries and Letters of Douglas Haig* (London: Weidenfeld and Nicolson, 2005). A scholarly presentation of a basic text for the Western Front, generally taking the side of the man who won the war.

Paul F Braim, *The Test of Battle: the American Expeditionary Forces in the Meuse-Argonne Campaign* (first published 1987; new edn, Shippensburg, PA: White Mane Books, 1998). A detailed account of the AEF's achievement that is prepared to be critical where necessary.

Anthony Bruce, *An Illustrated Companion to the First World War* (London: Michael Joseph, 1989). The next best thing to a 'dictionary' of the Great War, although it misses out the poets and gets tediously technical about different varieties of aircraft and ships.

151

The Great War on the Western Front

Stephen Bull, *Stosstrupptaktik, the First Stormtroopers* (Stroud, Gloucs: Spellmount, 2007). A welcome modern account of an important subject.

Rose E B Coombs, *Before Endeavours Fade: a Guide to the Battlefields of the First World War* (first published 1976; 6th edn, London: Battle of Britain Prints International, 1990). The first modern guidebook for the Western Front tourist, and still probably the best in a single volume. However, in recent years there has been an enthusiastic multiplication of more detailed guidebooks to individual battlefields, in step with the enthusiastic multiplication of battlefield tourists.

Michael Cox and John Ellis, *The World War I Databook* (London: Aurum Press, 1993). A modern presentation of facts and statistics.

Christopher Duffy, *Through German Eyes: the British and the Somme 1916* (London: Weidenfeld and Nicolson, 2006). A rare insight in English into how the Germans viewed their opponents on the Somme. On one side they found that many of the POW they captured expressed deep disaffection with their officers; on the other hand it is clear that the scale and force of the allied attack came as a very great setback to the Kaiser's men.

Paddy Griffith, *Battle Tactics of the Western Front: the British Army's Art of Attack, 1916–18* (New Haven and London: Yale University Press, 1994). An account of how the BEF improved its fighting methods towards the end of the war, following a painful process of trial and error.

Paddy Griffith, *Fortifications of the Western Front 1914–18* (Oxford: Osprey, 2004). A picture book illustrating how the techniques of fortification evolved.

Bruce Gudmundsson, *Stormtroop Tactics: Innovation in the German Army, 1914–18* (New York: Praeger, 1989). An excessively teutophile account which nevertheless lays out the (belated) development of German assault methods.

J P Harris, *Men, Ideas and Tanks: British Military Thought and Armoured Forces 1903–39* (Manchester: Manchester University Press, 1995). All the truth about tanks!

Further Reading

Paul Harris, *Amiens to the Armistice* (London: Brassey's, 1998). An excellent modern narrative of the 'Hundred Days' offensive, from 8 August to 11 November 1918.

Alistair Horne, *The Price of Glory* (London: Macmillan, 1962). The classic English-language account of the Verdun battle.

Peter Liddle (ed.), *Passchendaele in Perspective: the Third Battle of Ypres* (Barnsley: Leo Cooper, 1997). A wonderfully diverse collection of essays on this most controversial of all battles. Of particular note is John Hussey's account of the weather during the battle, which was a major determinant of the outcome.

Martin Middlebrook, *The First Day on the Somme* (London: Penguin, 1971). Microscopic dissection of the British army's worst day ever.

Martin Middlebrook, *The Kaiser's Battle* (London: Allen Lane, 1978). Microscopic dissection of the British army's second worst day.

Jonathan Nicholls, *Cheerful Sacrifice: the Battle of Arras 1917* (London: Leo Cooper, 1990). A fine account of an important battle that has somehow dropped out of public memory.

Terry Norman, *The Hell They Called High Wood* (London: Kimber, 1984). An illuminating narrative of the key fighting in the Somme battle that is often overlooked by those who think that 'the first day' was everything.

Barrie Pitt, *1918: the Last Act* (London: Cassell, 1962). Succinct and fast-moving account of the whole of 1918.

Robin Prior and Trevor Wilson, *Command on the Western Front* (Oxford: Blackwell, 1992). Ostensibly an account of the war as seen by General Rawlinson, this book led the way into the new generation of technical studies of how the battles were actually fought.

Julian Putkowski and Julian Sykes, *Shot at Dawn: Executions in World War One by Authority of the British Army Act* (London: Leo Cooper, 1989). The classic study at the heart of what has become a major subject-area in recent times.

Gary Sheffield and Dan Todman (eds), *Command and Control on the Western Front: the British Army's Experience, 1914–18* (London: Spellmount, 2004). A modern analysis of generalship.

The Great War on the Western Front

Leonard V Smith, *Between Mutiny and Obedience: the Case of the French Fifth Infantry Division during World War I* (New Jersey: Princeton University Press, 1994). It is only in very recent times that serious analyses of the French army's experiences have begun to appear in English. This sociological approach is one of the forerunners.

John Terraine, *The First World War 1914–18* (first published 1965; Papermac edn, 1984). An excellent succinct account.

Barbara Tuchman, *The Guns of August* (London: Random House, 1962). An accessible dissection of the complex manoeuvres that started the war.

Terence Zuber, *Inventing the Schlieffen Plan: German War Planning 1871–1914* (Oxford: Oxford University Press, 2002). A controversial modern analysis of just what Schlieffen did and did not actually plan, as well as the ways in which subsequent generations have tried to 'spin' it.

Autobiography and Literary Treatments

John Dos Passos, *Three Soldiers* (New York: Doran, 1921). A classic American view.

Brian Gardner (ed.), *Up the Line to Death: the War Poets 1914–18* (first published 1964; Magnum edn, London, 1977). A good anthology.

Robert Graves, *Goodbye to All That* (London: Jonathan Cape, 1929). The mould-breaking fictionalized (and semi-fictitious) account of a subaltern's experience on the Western Front, which opened the floodgates of 'protest' literature when it first appeared.

Ernest Hemingway, *A Farewell to Arms* (first published 1929; Penguin edn, London, 1966). A powerful novel of the Italian front, and war in general.

Ernst Jünger, *The Storm of Steel* (first English edn 1929; new edn, London: Constable, 1994). Remarkable autobiography of a thrusting German assault infantryman who believed in living dangerously. He collected twenty wounds in the Great War but survived as a German national hero for over a century.

Further Reading

Wilfred Owen, *Poems* (first published 1931; new edn, London: Chatto & Windus, 1946). The most remarkable distillation of the pity of war.

William St Clair, *The Road to St Julien: the Letters of a Stretcher-Bearer from the Great War*, ed. John St Clair (Barnsley: Leo Cooper, 2004). As great a rage against the war as anyone could wish, regrettably published only very recently.

Siegfried Sassoon, *Memoirs of an Infantry Officer* (first edn 1930; new edn, London: Faber & Faber, 1965). Memoirs complementing those of his friend Robert Graves, by an officer who sold himself further into the military ethos, and then sold himself further out of it.

Index

The Great War on the Western Front

Index